Things Get Hectic

Teens Write About the Violence That Surrounds Them

Youth Communication

Edited by
Philip Kay,
Andrea Estepa,
and Al Desetta

Foreword by Geoffrey Canada

A Touchstone Book
Published by Simon & Schuster

TOUCHSTONE
Rockefeller Center
1230 Avenue of the Americas
New York, NY 10020

Designed by Sam Potts
Manufactured in the United States of America

1 3 5 7 9 10 8 6 4 2

Library of Congress Cataloging-in-Publication Data
Things get hectic : teens write about the violence that surrounds them / Youth Communication ; edited by Philip Kay, Andrea Estepa, and Al Desetta ; foreword by Geoffrey Canada.
        p. cm.
"A Touchstone book."
1. Urban youth—United States. 2. Violence—United States. 3. Teenagers' writings, American. I. Kay, Philip. II. Estepa, Andrea. III. Desetta, Al. IV. Youth Communication (Organization)
                HQ796.T48 1998
305.235'0973—DC21   98-15115
                                              CIP

ISBN 0-684-83754-4

To my parents,
who tried to protect us.

P. K.

Contents

9 **Foreword**   *Geoffrey Canada*

13 **Introduction**   *Philip Kay*

Things Get Hectic

21 *When Things Get Hectic*   *Juan Azize*

26 *What Happened to*
   My American Dream?   *Natalie Neptune*

Home Is Where the Hurt Is: Abuse

33 *Letters to Parents*

35 *My Abused Friend: She Needs*
   More Help Than I Can Give   *Myriam Skye Holly*

41 *Home Is Where the Hurt Is*   *Zeena Bhattacharya*

49 *My Terrible Secret: Breaking the Silence*   *Anonymous*

6 Contents

53   *No One Spoke Up for Irma*   *Ana Angélica Pines*

59   *A Proud Moment:*

      Reporting the Abuse Upstairs   *Jessica Cabassa*

The Mind Slowly Begins to Defrost: Loss

63   *Will There Ever Be Justice for David?*   *Grismaldy Laboy*

72   *Maribel Feliciano: She Died*

      in the Arms of a Friend   *Adrian Jefferson*

75   *His Sneakers, My Dreams*   *Suzanne Joblonski*

77   *Remembering Mike*   *Carlos Lavezzari*

79   *No One Deserves to Die Like That*   *Wunika Hicks*

82   *How I Made Peace with the Past*   *Paula M. Verma*

The Culture of Violence

89   *Why I Love Gangsta Rap*   *J. Slade Anderson*

91   *Women Are Under a Rap Attack*   *Yelena Dynnikov*

94   *Diving into the Pit:*

      I Came, I Saw, I Moshed   *Allen Francis*

99   *Gaybashers: What Are They*

      Trying to Prove?   *Meliska Gruenler*

102   *The Media War Against Arabs*   *Mohamad Bazzi*

105   *Violent Times, Violent Movies*   *Daniel Jean-Baptiste*

108   *Hoods n' the Boys*   *Karina Sang-Petrillo*

A Gassed-Up Head Is Dangerous: Choices

113   *Letters to Parents*

115   *We Wanted Revenge*   *Carlos López*

Contents

117   *A Proud Moment: Turning In a Killer*   *Anonymous*

119   *Why I Carry a Gun*   *Anonymous*

122   *Why I Don't Have a Gun*   *Anonymous*

125   *I Carry Mace . . . Just in Case*   *Anonymous*

128   *My Secret Habit*   *Anonymous*

132   *I Hated Myself*   *David Miranda*

141   *Racking, Bombing, Tagging . . .*

      My Career as a Writer   *Anonymous*

146   *No More Clubbing for Me*   *Fabayo McIntosh*

149   *Karate Killed the Monster in Me*   *Robin K. Chan*

A Bull's-Eye on My Body: The Culture of Sexual Assault

157   *Tired of Being a Target*   *Loretta Chan*

161   *Why Guys Talk Nasty*   *Nanci S. Paltrowitz*

164   *Tell Him Why*   *Lisa Frederick*

The Price of Love: Boys, Girls, and Violence

169   *Letters to Parents*

171   *I Paid a High Price for Love*   *Melissa Krolewski*

177   *He Won't Stop Hitting Me*   *Anonymous*

180   *Dream Guy, Nightmare Experience*   *Anonymous*

185   *My Love, My Friend, My Enemy*   *Anonymous*

196   *I Never Thought He'd Try to Kill Me*   *Anonymous*

202   *The Anger Can Go Somewhere Else*   *Anonymous*

Cops and Kids

207   *Reaction to the Anthony Baez Verdict*

210   *Cops and Kids*   Reported by Julio A. Garcia

214   *Caught in the Act*   Rance Scully

216   *Rikers: Frontin' for Respect*   José R.

220   *Busted*   Ligeia Minetta

Some Serious Déjà Vu: War Stories

233   *New York City Is Worlds Apart*
      from El Salvador   Norma E. López

236   *How My Family Escaped*
      the Nazis   Alison Stein Wellner

241   *My Escape from the Secret Police*   Hanify Ahmed

246   *The L.A. Riots: Beirut*
      All Over Again   Mohamad Bazzi

249   *Operation Paintball:*
      Splattering the Enemy   Julio Pagan

253   *My Summer in the Israeli Army*   Melissa Chapman

257   *Letter to an Iraqi Mother*
      and Other Student Reactions to the Gulf War

261   *The Price of War*

263   *No Parades for One Bronx Family*   Sheila Maldonado

271   **Guide to Essays**
275   **Acknowledgments**
277   **About Youth Communication**
281   **About the Editors**

Foreword

Geoffrey Canada

One afternoon a few years ago my pager went off and, when I went to the phone, it was one of my students imploring me to come quickly; her brother Ronald had been injured in a fight. Another boy had smashed a bottle over his head, slashing his head and face, and he was in the emergency room at St. Luke's Hospital. Ronald was very special to me, like my own son. I dropped what I was doing and dashed right over there. I knew the silent group of boys waiting outside; I had helped raise most of them. They told me Ronald was inside. Another kid had "snuck" him when he wasn't looking. There was something in their tone, something in their body language, that disturbed me, but it didn't register right away.

Ronald was in the midst of an inner-city emergency room nightmare. People everywhere were bleeding, moaning, and waiting to be seen by a doctor. I talked my way into the room in which Ronald was being treated and saw him lying on a gurney with several huge gashes in his forehead and face. The attending physician told me they were short of help and he was still in the process of cleaning the glass out of the wound. I told him I would help. He began to clean and I began to talk. I knew if I could get Ronald talking he would be distracted and the process would be less painful. I asked him what happened and he told me. But in the telling he was so distant, so coldly straightforward, that I realized I was not talking to the boy I knew and raised. I was talking to a boy who had been transformed into something I had never known him to be—a killer! Ronald was preparing to kill the boy who had injured him. What tipped me off? It was a certain look in his eyes, an emotional detachment. Ronald had covered up his wounds and his pain with the certainty of getting revenge. And what an awful revenge it would be. I wondered if I could pierce that detachment and get to the deep well of pain that he had covered up. Could I open up *that* wound and help Ronald survive the hurt, the anger, the hatred, and thus save his life?

The book you are about to read contains the raw truth about the pain and violence many young people like Ronald face every day. It is a truth that is different from the one I knew growing up in the South Bronx in the late fifties. There was violence then, but not the casual homicidal violence of today that has claimed tens of thousands of our teens. There was pain and teenage angst, but there was also a community of family and neighbors to help heal young hearts and spirits. *Things Get Hectic* gives us a first-hand account of what every parent, teacher, youth worker, and caring adult must know about. We can no longer close our eyes or our hearts to the violence that our youth are forced to live with. It costs us too much as a society not to care. We pay in many ways: the wasted lives, the cost of incarceration, the taxes lost from those too damaged to work. And if we allow our youth to continue to live in such a violent world without trying to help them, we will not only lose this country's future but part of our own souls as well.

After reading this book you may find your worldview slightly altered. This is not a bad thing. It was only when I finally under-stood the violence that my young people were living, day in and day out, that I began to see opportunities to help them, to save them. Seeing things from their point of view is like putting on glasses that let you see a whole world that you couldn't have seen otherwise. There are signs that are obvious, actions that seem inevitable, moments that are crucial in lives that are teeter-ing on the brink of disaster. But unless you understand the con-text that young people live in today, it's all easy to miss.

It took a long time to get Ronald back from the brink. It wasn't just the pain of the wound, it was the injustice, the scars for life, the code of the street that told him, "For every action there is an unequal action, more hurtful, more painful," and "Rather be dead or in jail for murder than face the years of pain alone." But Ronald was not alone—I was there. Together we cried and cursed and be-gan to heal one another. When I was sure that the murderous rage had been bled from his heart, I went outside to wait for Ronald to be released. His friends were still there. Still waiting. Suddenly it hit me: I knew what I was seeing in their eyes, their body lan-guage. I had just seen the same look Ronald's eyes—murder! Now here it was again. They wanted to kill. I had known these boys most of their lives and yet now they were strangers to me. I went to Alonso, who I knew was the leader. I told him loud enough so that all could hear that there would be no murder, this night or any other. I would personally go to the police and turn them all in. I called each one by name so that they would know I had seen them all. I yelled my threats. They turned their backs and cursed me under their breath.

In the end, there was no revenge killing. In many ways I got the boys off the hook. They were able to say to themselves and to one another that they would have sought revenge, but Geoff would have turned them in to the police if they had. Ronald is now a fine young man working for a living. Alonso is in college, and the other boys are doing fine. Later I realized that they were all trapped—trapped in a culture of violence that they felt dic-tated all the rules. I almost missed all the clues that they were about to make a decision at 14 that would have ruined their lives forever. I listen more closely now.

Want to know what young people are living with every day? Want to understand how to help? *Things Get Hectic* will tell you with brutal honesty what our children face growing up today. They want us to know. It is in trying to understand the lives of our youth that we learn what we must do to save them. From these stories come answers to questions we have not asked, but should. First we must listen, then we must act.

Introduction

by Philip Kay

On December 15, 1994, a firebomb exploded on a subway train underneath Lenox Avenue in Harlem, severely burning 13-year-old Arnell Austin. Police initially suspected that Kamron Warren, 16, who was also injured in the blast, had been carrying the device in her bookbag when it accidentally went off. They would not speculate as to the motive, and their suspicions later turned out to have been unfounded. At the time, however, few people who heard the news seemed to find it doubtful or peculiar that a girl Kamron's age would be involved in a crime of that nature, and that was perhaps inevitable. By the early 1990s, violent behavior on the part of young people—particularly as it was being portrayed in the news media—had already become so savage and pervasive that allegations like these scarcely raised an eyebrow anymore. Just three months earlier, a 13-year-old had been arrested for killing four people in the firebombing of a Bronx grocery store. And not long before that, a group of teens was charged with setting a homeless man on fire as he slept in a local park. Meanwhile, the number of gun homicides involving adolescents nationwide had nearly quintupled, and words like "wolfpack," "drive-by," and "9-millimeter" had become a part of Americans' everyday speech.

Children growing up in this kind of climate confront a host of terrifying experiences and palpable threats. They live with a constant sense of menace in their homes, schools, and neighborhoods and often suffer the sudden, wrenching loss of friends, family members, and cultural heroes. And they have to make tough choices about how to survive. *Things Get Hectic* is a collection of stories, letters, and essays by more than fifty such young people who have come of age in a particularly vicious period in our history. The book begins in a neighborhood in Queens, New York, where a dirty look between two strangers leads to a spray of gunfire and teenagers armed with box cutters and hammers send one another to the hospital without really understanding why. It ends in the South Bronx apartment of a woman who has just lost a son to "friendly fire" in the Persian Gulf War. Along the way, there are firsthand accounts by teens who are in the midst of dealing with beatings and rapes by parents and boyfriends.

Their stories have a rare kind of immediacy. We're right there in the room with 15-year-old Grismaldy Laboy as she gets the news of her cousin's murder and again when word comes that his accused killer has been acquitted of all charges. We hear how, for 21-year-old Wunika Hicks, the murder of a favorite rap star conjures up memories of watching her own father gunned down in the street and the near-total disintegration of her family that followed. We also meet teens who do violence to themselves, attempting suicide or sticking their fingers down their throats after every meal, and others who take their frustrations out on unsuspecting strangers. The writers discuss the physical and verbal assaults they endure daily at the hands of strangers on the street, police officers, and people in the media and the different ways they themselves have flirted with violent behavior.

The teenagers' individual responses to these kinds of experiences are every bit as varied as the experiences themselves. Ana Pines decides not to alert the authorities about the way her friend's mother is abusing her. "Why should the adults at the [child welfare] hotline be any different from the ones on my block?" she concludes. But confronted with a similar situation, Jessica Cabassa ignores her mother's advice to "leave it alone" and calls the cops. Where one writer defends his decision to carry a gun, another decides that owning one would only make him feel invincible and render him even more vulnerable in the end. Yet another opts to arm herself with chemical Mace only after a long discussion with her mother of the attendant fears, risks, and benefits.

Not all their choices involve weapons, revenge, or despair, however. Allen Francis attends an alternative-rock concert so that he can experience slam dancing. Julio Pagan travels upstate with his buddies and shoots "the enemy" with paint pellets from expensive toy rifles. And Melissa Chapman spends the summer training with the Israeli army. For others, writing graffiti and taking karate lessons provide an outlet for their rage. "It was like I was exploding for all the times I kept quiet to avoid an argument or backed down from a fight," Allen tells us.

Through their tales of victimization, survival, and resilience, these young writers show the determination to rise above their environments. "I knew from experience that there were already enough evil and menacing people in this world," writes 15-year-old Robin Chan. "I didn't want to become one of them." Their stories are peppered with scathing critiques of the world they're forced to grow up in. "As long as they kept us quiet, the adults could pretend the problem didn't exist," they tell us. No one knows better than teenagers how thoughtlessly or hypocritically we adults are capable of behaving, nor is anyone more eager to set us straight. The writers also denounce state-sponsored violence wherever they find it, whether it comes from world leaders like George Bush and Saddam Hussein or from local law enforcement personnel like the officers who brutalized Rodney

King or the one who put a choke hold on Anthony Baez for playing touch football too close to his patrol car. When 16-year-old Natalie Neptune, who's just about ready to file her application for U.S. citizenship, hears about the police allegedly torturing Abner Louima, she's not sure if she likes what becoming an American stands for. "Why should I be part of this country," she asks, "if I have to fear the people who are supposed to protect me just like my parents feared the police in Haiti?"

The incidents recounted here are dramatic enough, but much of what the stories have to offer is not in the events themselves but in the telling. Suzanne Joblonski writes about "Sam," a young man who sits next to her in criminal justice class (and on whom she seems to have a slight crush). When Sam fails to show up one Monday morning, Suzanne learns that he was shot and killed over the weekend, apparently over a pair of sneakers. But she doesn't merely give us a soundbite about how disturbing that was. She provides her own frame for the experience—how the young man wanted to go into the military, for example, and ultimately become a corrections officer, how others in the class wanted to become cops, lawyers, and social workers. There are no budding teachers, artists, or engineers here—even before Sam is killed they already seem to have imagined their futures as falling on one side or another of some kind of war. And Suzanne's message for Sam's teenage killers is strangely compassionate: Plan ahead. Find something to look forward to.

In another moving story of the death of a schoolmate, a young woman named Yvette describes watching the fatal stabbing of her best friend, Maribel, on the subway ride home from school. "I remember when I was younger and I asked my mother why, in the movies, people spat up blood," says Yvette, "and she said it meant they were dead. That's how I knew Maribel was dead." How many of those of us who came of age in the 1960s and 1970s were watching movies in which people spit up blood before we were old enough to understand what that meant? On the one hand, such movies may have helped prepare Yvette to cope with her friend's death. On the other, the confusion and terror instilled by a lifetime of being bombarded by those same images may have helped Maribel's young assailant feel the need to strike first.

Which brings us back to Kamron Warren, the 16-year-old whose bookbag suspiciously exploded in flames that afternoon on the #3 train. It wasn't until a week after the incident, when another, bigger bomb exploded on a train underneath New York's financial district, that investigators determined the original device had in fact been planted by Edward J. Leary, a 49-year-old unemployed computer consultant from suburban New Jersey. Suspecting Kamron was an unfortunate mistake, but given the extent of youth violence in our cities, a mistake almost anybody could have made.

The one mistake we must never permit ourselves to make, however, is to underestimate the toll violence takes on young people's psyches, their schoolwork, and their friendships—not to mention the kinds of self-destructive behavior it leads them to. If we learn nothing else from the teenagers in this book, it's that every time a bomb or a handgun goes off in the vicinity of a child in this country it's because adults, directly or indirectly, helped put it there. We all helped create the material conditions that made it possible for that to happen, and all of us have failed in our communal responsibility to provide a safe world for our children to grow up in. Violence is not about age or hormones or genetics. It's a response people of all ages and cultures learn and internalize over a lifetime and, with a little support from their communities, one they have it within themselves to unlearn and overcome.

The press didn't seem to take much of an interest in how the third-degree burns on young Arnell Austin's legs were healing or how Kamron, her family, and her friends felt about the false allegations that had been leveled against her. As a society, we seem to be primarily concerned about the damage teenagers like these have the potential to inflict on us. If we ever want to do something about violence in America, we should begin by trying to understand what it is like to be 13 years old and have to ride the #3 train to and from school every day with bombs going off all around you.

Editors' Note: The stories in this book were written in the decade between 1987 and 1997 and, with a few exceptions, were originally published in the teen-written magazine New Youth Connections. *For original publication dates, see page 267.*

Things Get Hectic

When Things Get Hectic

By Juan Azize

Last summer I was headed to the bodega around my block to get a hero when I saw my boy Deps step to some kid I'd never seen before. Being the nosy friend that I am, I went over to see what the problem was. "Yo Deps, what's going on man?" I said.

"This b--ch ass n--ga got an eye problem," Deps answered.

"Whatever man," said the kid. I noticed he got scared when I came over, knowing there were two of us now and this wasn't his neighborhood.

But fighting over a bad look wasn't exactly the move. "Yo, forget about that sh-t man," I said. "He don't want no beef."

"So why he trying to scope if he don't want none?" said Deps.

"I wasn't scoping at you man," answered the kid.

"Yo man, squash this bullsh-t already so I could get my sandwich," I told Deps. "My stomach is growling."

"Aaiight man, just don't be trying to act like you represent around here," Deps told the kid. They gave each other the hand along with dirty looks and slow moves.

After the fake pound, I went inside the store to get my salami and cheese and Deps tagged along. About fifteen minutes later there we were chilling in front of my house. It was really hot and we were trying to throw girls in front of the hydrant and munching down that delicious hero when, all of a sudden, a blue Corolla with tinted windows rolled up in front of us.

I knew right away this was the kid Deps was riffing to. I remember the hero losing its delicious taste. The girls were still teasing us, trying to get us to chase them, when Deps tapped my leg cause he knew what time it was. Before I could yell "duck," I saw the back window roll down enough for a gun to fit through. I grabbed Deps like a reflex and we both hit the floor at the same time two bullets hit the side of my house.

The car was long gone before me and Deps had a chance to feel burnt. All of a sudden the girls didn't want to play anymore and it wasn't that sunny. I never knew things could get to that point so fast. A dirty look setting bullets off didn't make any sense. What if they had caught us from behind? What if they had shot one of the girls? What if my mother had been standing there?

It really made me think deep. I wanted to kill those guys, I was so steamed. I was confused. I was flipping. I rode around with my friends looking for that blue Corolla for that whole week. Deps got a gun that same day hoping they were going to come back, which didn't happen.

This kind of thing goes on all the time: "Yo, you heard who got shot?" "I ran into some beef today." "Yo man, bring a shank just in case." I am sick and tired of hearing it. Violence surrounds us everywhere: school, work, even in front of your crib. That's the number one reason for deaths among teens in New York City. Kids nowadays are ready to kill each other over the dumbest things.

I know a lot of kids who are scared one day they are just going to get blasted for something stupid like that. There are so many other kids out there with guns, knives, and short tempers.

I live in Corona, Queens, and when the weekends come I feel like I am in a battle zone. Before trooping it out to a jam I always have to make sure I am rolling with my little crew in case things get hectic. Most of the jams I've been to end up with a shootout or a rumble.

And this stuff doesn't just go down where I live. In school all the gossip in the hallway is about things happening in the streets. I know lots of people also carry weapons to school but the beef is outside most of the time.

There was this time, last year in my old school, when my boy Duzer was supposed to shoot a fair one with another kid in school, so my little crew got together to keep it a fair fight. When eighth period came we all hit the handball courts. While Duzer hopped around to get ready, I saw kids pulling shanks and hammers out of their JanSports. I knew this wasn't going to be no fair fight, fake gangstas put that out of style trying to find the easy way out.

It started to get hectic; people were getting shanked up and hammered down. I was playing it safe and taking them sucker punches every chance I had. It was an even rumble, not counting the fact that they had more weapons. (I admit I was scared to death about them hammers.)

When the 5-0's rolled up we were gone with the wind. A couple of kids couldn't run so they stayed on the floor covering their sore spots. My boy Eliester had a thin slice on his neck and had to get eleven stitches. The rest of us had shanked jackets and arms, nothing serious (thank God).

We ran to the hospital about ten blocks away. About a half hour later, after the hype went down, I stopped Duzer in the waiting room and asked him what the beef was all about. I almost started to laugh when I heard the answer: "He was trying to tell me who I wasn't allowed to talk to," answered Duzer. "Yo, I was up on that b--ch way before that n--ga even dreamed about it."

A girl! I didn't understand. One of our boys gets sliced in the neck with eleven stitches and three other kids were left on the floor bleeding like cold. This sh-t was pathetic, killing each other over a girl who's probably ready to move on to the next man. Eight-tracks make better sense than that.

I look at it this way: If I am going to have beef I am going to have beef worth having. Not over a girl, a bad skeem, a stupid remark, or any other petty things. I am going to make sure before I go all out that it's for a good cause. What is a good cause for me? Somebody trying to kill me, rob me, or anybody that touches my mother.

Besides that, you got to keep it real. The last thing in your mind should be a Glock or a blackjack, that's all unnecessary violence. Nobody has to go that far unless it is life threatening. There are many kids out there who only get down when they are strapped or rolling deep. Remember, the real people won't need that when they blow your finesse. And you aren't always going to have your gun or your crew to hide behind. Slow down or it's going to happen when you are not looking.

You should only try to get respect if disrespected, without letting things get out of hand. I'm not saying it's easy, trust me. Nowadays there is no respect, everyone wants to be bigger than the next guy. But real people keep it real. They are the ones that go all with their hands and not with their guns, knowing it will give them both a chance to come back. Like that rap song goes: "Leave your nines at home and bring your skills to the battle."

We should all try to calm down. Violence won't solve anything in the long run. We have to grow up and realize there are other ways to solve a problem—talking it out and mediating and sometimes even ignoring it. We've got to try to remember a lot of kids are getting killed over little problems that could have been easily solved.

I am not gonna front, though. If my boys get into more senseless beef, I am still going to catch their backs and I won't stop to ask them what the problem is. Adrenaline flows faster than questions, and my boys have always been there for me when I needed them without asking questions and trying to talk it out.

I guess it must be written in that invisible book that knows everything, the one where ladies go first and actions speak louder than words. The funny thing is, I follow that book. If my boys have beef again I'll be there asking mute questions that come out too late. It's like a reflex. It shouldn't be, but it is. Your boys are your boys. I do stop to think about it, but only after it's too late, after the damage is already done.

In the past three years, I've lost three of my boys to senseless violence. Every time it happens, the rest of us get together and make a mural on the wall. For me, the hardest part is figuring out what colors and design to use. How are we supposed to concentrate without the whole crew? Even the invisible book doesn't have an answer to that one. It doesn't have a special chapter on consequences.

We all have one life to live, let's keep it real. Cause I am tired of trying to figure out colors and designs for my friends' memorials. Wouldn't you be?

This goes out to SEN and to all those who have fallen to violence. Rest In Peace. Nobody is ever promised tomorrow. Increase the peace.

What Happened to My American Dream?

By Natalie Neptune

I was born on January 25, 1981, on a boat traveling from Haiti to America. When my father first told me I was born in the ocean, I thought I must be a mermaid, and I couldn't understand why I didn't turn into one when I took a bath. Then he explained that I was born on a boat.

My parents came here on that boat in search of a better life. They wanted to leave a country where the police could beat you up for no reason or break into your house, where they raped the women and mutilated the men. As I've grown up, they've told me horror stories of things the police in Haiti have done to their friends. They came to America hoping that things would be different for them and for their children.

Although I've spent my entire life in this country and have never once been to Haiti, officially I am a Haitian citizen. A few months ago, when my parents became American citizens, I decided that I wanted to become one too.

My parents became citizens because of new laws being passed that would cut off or strictly limit aid to non-Americans living in this country. They also thought it would help them bring my older brother, Jean, here to live with us.

My parents told me that becoming a citizen would help me get money for college. But for me becoming a citizen seemed like the first step in fulfilling my American dream. I imagined becoming a successful writer and moving out of my neighborhood, where there are so many crackheads and fences everywhere, moving some place with houses and green grass. I wanted to do what my parents did, sacrifice for a better future.

After my parents became citizens, my mother gave me their citizenship papers to hold on to and I put them in a drawer in my desk. Whenever my parents went out, I would take the papers out and look at them. To see my parents' certificates was great, but it hurt not to see my name on them. For months I nagged my parents to get me the proper forms so I could become a citizen too. On a Saturday night in July, my father finally came home with them.

I thought that when the papers finally arrived, I would be doing cartwheels with excitement. I was happy to get the forms, but in the months that I waited, I began to have second thoughts.

Over the summer while I was working at *New Youth Connections,* I traveled into Manhattan regularly for the first time in my life, and I began to notice the way Black people and other minorities worked in the little jobs—behind the counter or cleaning up the parks—while the White people hurried off to offices in suits and ties. I wondered why almost all the cabdrivers were Indian, Black, or Middle Eastern, while almost all the passengers were White.

I began to be bothered by the fact that there aren't that many Black people in positions of power. I felt angry that politicians want to throw juvenile offenders into adult jails while cutting money out of school budgets. I worried that for Blacks and minorities like myself, the American dream could turn into an American nightmare.

Then, a few days after I received my citizenship papers, I saw an article in the *Daily News* about a man named Abner Louima who was allegedly beaten and raped with a toilet plunger by cops of the 70th Precinct. I felt sick to my stomach. The police officers were given the job to protect and serve the people of this country, but instead they were trying to kill this man.

The details of the beating and torture were so graphic—by the time Louima was finally taken to the hospital, he had damaged internal organs and broken teeth—that at first I didn't want to read any more. I was so mad I just wanted to see the cops receive the same treatment they had given Louima.

In the evening when I got home, I read the article more carefully. It was then that I realized that Abner Louima was Haitian. If he had been African-American or Chinese, I still would have been upset. Any time someone is robbed of his dignity and self-respect, I'm angry. But when I read that he was Haitian and heard on the radio that racist remarks were allegedly made by the police, that really pissed me off. It reminded me of rude things I had heard about Haitians before and I questioned whether I wanted to become a citizen at all.

In the summer of 1992, a brutal military regime was ruling Haiti and Haitians were fleeing to this country in great numbers.

Many settled in New York and at that time I heard people in my neighborhood, both Black and White, stereotyping Haitians, calling us "boat people," making fun of how we spoke English, saying that you would get AIDS if you slept with a Haitian woman.

I watched on the news how Haitians—including my own aunt and uncle—were being held prisoner at the Guantánamo Bay naval base in Cuba in overcrowded conditions just because they were trying to save themselves and seek refuge in America.

When I heard that Louima had been beaten by the police and harassed because he was Haitian, I remembered all these things, and questions filled my mind. Why should I be part of a country that doesn't want to open its arms to people who seek refuge here? Why should I be part of this country if I have to fear the people who are supposed to protect me just like my parents feared the police in Haiti?

If it hadn't been for the Louima case, I probably would have filled out the forms anyway and become a citizen. Now, though, I've decided to wait. I guess I feel a little hopeless, and I just don't believe that I can change this country. I don't see anyone I would want to vote for or anyone who thinks like me.

I want to become an American citizen for the right reasons—I don't just want to do it so I can get government aid for college or for some other financial benefits. I want to feel passionate about my country and I want to feel like I can bring about change.

Maybe in a few years I'll feel differently. If I do become a citizen, I hope I'll use that power to fight to eliminate some of the problems that I see going on now.

Right now, though, in light of what happened to Abner Louima, I'm just not ready to fill out the forms and declare that I'm part of this country.

Home Is Where the Hurt Is

Abuse

Letters to Parents

Dear Mom,

   The reason I left home when I was 16 is not that I don't love you. I love you very much. I left home because Dad was always beating me, punching on me when he got drunk and threatening to kill me if I ever told you.

   While he was beating me, he used to tell me that I'm always coming between you and him. He told me once that every time he turns away I'm always trying to get you away from him.

   I have scars on my back and the upper back of my legs from the beatings he gave me. I never showed you these scars or told you about him hitting me, because I thought he was going to kill me if I did.

   Up until his death six months ago, I couldn't say anything about this because I thought if I did he would find me and kill me.

   I know he loved you and I know you loved him, but I don't

feel any remorse over his death. I feel relieved. I feel safe now that he is gone and I can tell you why I left home.

I would like to come and see you soon. Oh, by the way, Mom, I got a surprise for you. I'll be bringing my fiancée with me.

Frankie (name changed)

Dear Dad,

How are you? Fine, I hope. I know we haven't seen each other in about ten years and now I want you back in my life. I really wish you had been here in my early life, because a lot of things happened to me.

First, I would like to talk about my so-called stepdad. From when I was 7 years old until I was 10, he used to touch me in places that made me very uncomfortable. From the time I turned 10 until I was 14, he used to have sex with me when I would come home from school and no one was there.

I always felt that it was my fault when it happened to me. I couldn't tell my mom, and still can't, because she just wouldn't understand. She isn't very talkative or understanding like you. Besides, she's always at work or church, too busy to know what's going on.

I wish that you could have come and taken me away from all of the pain I had to endure. I often asked myself why you left. Was it because you didn't like me or because I did something wrong? Can you please tell me? I love you and wish you could come and see me.

I was married and have a son but his father and I don't get along because he tells me what to do. We are always fighting and now I live in a shelter and attend school and my son is in day care. Sometimes I get really stressed and don't know what to do. Can you come to New York so we can talk? I'll be waiting to hear from you.

**Love always,
Your Daughter**

My Abused Friend: She Needs More Help Than I Can Give

By Myriam Skye Holly

Some of the names in this story have been changed.

When we were little kids, my friend Carmen always told me how her mother would beat her after she did something wrong. At first, I just figured that she was getting "disciplined" like everyone else. It wasn't until one morning when I was 6 that I found out the truth.

Carmen lives pretty close, so we'd walk to school together. When I got to her house, Carmen's mother was brushing her hair into a ponytail. She redid that same ponytail maybe three or four times, causing Carmen to get restless. Mrs. Nichols started yelling that Carmen wasn't sitting up straight, and was going to make her late for work because of all the time she was spending on Carmen's hair. Then she pulled my friend up by the hair and hit her in the face with the hairbrush.

Carmen sucked her teeth in at her mother and got a hard slap across the face. Even though I was only 6, I knew that this wasn't right. Mrs. Nichols finished with Carmen's hair and told her to hurry on to school. As Carmen packed her schoolbag, her mother gently smiled at me. "Good morning, Myriam," she said and walked over to her bedroom.

Walking to school, I asked Carmen if she felt okay, and she nodded. "I told you," she said a little later. And that was all.

As the years passed, the beatings have only increased in number and gotten more severe. Mr. Nichols cheats on his wife and has another child. Because he's physically stronger than she is and has been known to beat her really badly, she takes her problems with him out on Carmen. Sometimes you can hear yelling and crying coming from the house and, if the light is on in her bedroom, occasionally you'll see Carmen's mother moving around, trying to hit her.

This situation is probably the hardest thing in my life. I feel helpless and I never really know what to do. What can I do? What can I do that I know will work out and truly benefit my friend? I'm not sure and neither is she.

As I've gotten older, I've tried different ways to help my friend deal with this situation. Whether it's an ear to listen, a shoulder to cry on, or words to comfort, I always try to be there for her any way I can.

Sometimes Carmen will say that if she didn't have friends over after school who drank all the juice in the refrigerator or other things like that, then her mom wouldn't get so mad and hit her. I always try to let her know that she isn't responsible for her mother's actions and shouldn't feel guilty. It isn't her fault that her mother and father's problems always seem to come down on her. I tell her that I think her mother still loves her, she just doesn't know how to deal with her problems. (Although sometimes I have a hard time believing that.)

But what I think really helps her the most is my just listening to her explain what happens each time and let her feelings out, something she's not allowed to do at home—it's considered "backtalk."

Now that Carmen is 14, her mom will call her a "tramp" and mean names just because a lot of older guys who she doesn't give the time of day notice her. I advise her not to argue with her mother for whatever reason—even if she knows her mother is wrong and she has a deep desire to yell back at her.

Because of her anger at her mother, whenever people at school give Carmen problems or get jealous of her and talk behind her back, she'll fight them. And since she can really bust ass, she's the one who gets in trouble and gets her mother called in for a parent conference, a poor conduct grade, and usually a suspension (not to mention another beating).

Recently, I told her to release her emotions through writing because that has always worked for me. Although she previously hated writing, she likes it more now, and frequently writes her "memoir essays," as she calls them, and some poetry.

Meanwhile, the beatings continue. If I'm around when it's happening I try to stop it. Sometimes I'll try talking to Mrs. Nichols right then and there. Because she is usually convinced that Carmen is to blame, I'll apologize for her. I'll say that Carmen didn't mean it and that everything is going to be okay and will work itself out. I hate to lie, but I think I sound pretty convincing.

Other times I'll approach her in the most indirect way possible so she won't think her daughter put me up to it or that we're plotting something against her. (I don't want Carmen to get wrecked after I leave.) I'll start off saying, "How are you doing today, Mrs. Nichols? . . . Yeah, that's nice. . . . Yes, I'm doing okay in school. . . ." Then I ask her how she feels about the bad things that are going on with her husband and whether she really feels Carmen is responsible. I'll ask her if she really thinks "getting mad" will change anything.

I try to let her know that this really bothers her daughter and I make it really clear that Carmen still loves her, maybe to soften up her heart a little. She never says whether she will stop or not but, because we get along so well, at least she's willing to listen and even admit in the most indirect way that it is a problem.

But most of the time Mrs. Nichols only says that Carmen was "trying to act bright with me," and that the beatings "just happen." I'm sorry; black eyes, swollen cheeks, and overflowing tears don't just happen, not in my opinion.

Several times I've tried to find places for Carmen to stay

where she'd be safe and away from her mother. I tried hooking her up with friends and relatives on Long Island. Although Carmen wanted to get away, she always refuses to go for fear that her mother will find a way to get back at her for trying something like running away.

Carmen always gets scared when taking a step toward solving the problem. She feels that there isn't any solution and that she'll just have to live with it until she's older and can get out of the house and get her revenge.

One day last spring, after Mrs. Nichols woke her up in the middle of the night and hit her because she was upset that Mr. Nichols was getting home late, Carmen finally decided that she'd had enough. She came to school the next day with her left cheek all swollen. She was real distant in class and everyone could tell that she didn't want to talk about it so nobody really pressed her for information.

Not until later in the day did Daquan (another friend who tries to help her sometimes) and I try talking about it.

"What's up, Carmen? You all right?" Daquan asked. "What happened wit you moms?"

"Oh, she was just whackin' my ass from three in the mornin' because my daddy came home late," she replied.

"Do you want me to get some ice for your cheek, Carmen?" I asked. "Or get some cocoa butter from my bag?"

"No, it's okay, y'all. I'm just feelin' real dizzy. I need to go home."

But Daquan said, "That's f--ked up though, cuz she there now."

I suggested that Carmen go to the nurse's office and lie down for the rest of the day. But she said she was fed up with "all this sh-t" and decided to talk to Mrs. Buckley, a school guidance counselor. Daquan and I walked Carmen to the office. Carmen explained what had been going on and, without telling Carmen what she was planning to do, Mrs. Buckley called her mother. She told Carmen's mother that she was aware of the problem and gave her some kind of warning, I believe. Carmen arrived home that afternoon to find her mother prepared to whip her for what she'd done.

Needless to say, Carmen felt betrayed and gave up whatever hope she might have had of trying to take any kind of action. A couple of months later, I was walking down the block one evening and heard Carmen crying hysterically up in her room. Her aunt let me in and muttered something about Carmen's mom "hurting that girl." I went upstairs and Mrs. Nichols was in the hall with the most peculiar look on her face. It was like this half-sad, half-mad expression. When she's beating up on Carmen she's always mad but this time it was different. It was as if she was beginning to feel sorry for Carmen and regret what she'd done. I asked her how she was, although a part of me wanted to smack her.

"All right, Myriam," she said. "It's just Carmen. You know how she is—never listening, trying to act bright with me. I didn't want to, but she just . . . oh, you know, it just happened."

Standing outside Carmen's bedroom door, I braced myself. I closed my eyes for a second and prayed it wouldn't be as bad as I thought it might be.

It was even worse. It had never been like this before. Carmen was sitting on her bed with her beautiful hair all in her face. She didn't have that usual distant look that she gets and she wasn't trying to act like nothing happened. She was just crying and crying. I went over to her and slowly, painfully pushed her hair from her face and pulled it back into a ponytail. It was hard to look directly at her. Her left eye was swollen shut and she had black and reddish bruises all over her face. The right side of her nose was scratched and there were little marks all up and down her arms and a cut on her left knee.

My heart was breaking for her and I think it was my crying that finally got her to stop. She just sat there perfectly still with the most distant look on her face that I've ever seen on anyone.

I went to the kitchen to make her some peppermint tea because she always says that makes her feel better inside. This time I had to force her to drink it. Then she finally told me what happened. It seems Mrs. Nichols had told Carmen to wash her hair only on a certain day of the week so she wouldn't use up all the shampoo in the house. Now Carmen is very conscious of her looks, especially her hair, and she washed it anyway. Carmen said that when her mom came home and saw that the shampoo was finished she slapped her all over her body, punched her repeatedly in the face, kicked her and pulled her around by the hair, whacking her in the face with a vacuum cleaner attachment. She wrecked Carmen up so bad. I didn't even think Mrs. Nichols had that much strength in her. She seems so fragile herself.

After she finished telling me what happened, Carmen blurted out, "I'm going to call Child Welfare on that b--ch, so that they can make her pay!" Child Welfare (CWA) is the agency that deals with child abuse. We'd talked about it before. We didn't really know what it was going to do but we just felt that it might get something started toward finding a way out. Once I even handed her the phone but she wouldn't go through with it because she was afraid her mother would find a way to get back at her. This time it was the same thing.

She said that she didn't want to talk about it anymore and we went to the living room and watched MTV. But neither one of us was really paying attention. I mean, how could we?

After that day, when Carmen would come to school all sad and beaten up, I'd accompany her to the nurse's office so she could lie down for the day. She'd rather do that than go back to a guidance counselor because she doesn't believe that would solve the problem. The counselor would probably only call her mother up again and then her mother would be waiting for her when she got home from school. "It's like I'm trapped," she once told me.

That night with the shampoo was the worst it's ever been. But Carmen says that she survived. "How much worse could it get?" she asked me.

The thing is that we both feel deep down that it is going to get a lot worse. Sometimes I worry that she'll wind up in a coma one day. Many times I feel that I should do more but I don't know what more I can do. So for now, I'll just be there to offer my ear and that peppermint tea that she likes. I just want Carmen to know that whenever she needs it, help from me is dependable. My ear, heart, mind, and door are always open.

Home Is Where the Hurt Is

By Zeena Bhattacharya

For the first ten years of my life I lived with my grandparents in Calcutta, India. I didn't know my parents at all. Then, one spring afternoon, I came home from school and found my grandmother packing. "Are we going somewhere?" I asked. "Yes, to your parents, in Madras," she answered.

My parents had sent me to live with my grandparents when I was only a few days old. No one ever told me why. Nor did they tell me why we were going to see them now. Still, I had never been to Madras before and I was very excited about going to a new place.

I went to my grandfather and sat on his lap. "Is it true we are going to Madras?" I asked. Just for a moment, I thought I saw tears in his eyes. But he smiled and said, "Yes, I'm taking you there." Immediately I was reassured.

"Oh boy! I'm going to Madras—to M-A-D-R-A-S," I

shouted and ran out to tell my friends. Not once did it occur to me that my life with my grandparents was about to end.

At first, I found Madras very beautiful. It was like a big vacation for me and my grandfather with the two strange people I had only known from pictures. But after a month, my grandfather left. I was heartbroken—of all the people in the world, I loved and trusted him the most. How could he leave me with these people I had known for only a month? But I tried to make the best of it.

I tried to do everything my parents asked me to. They never really talked to me—just ordered me to do things or not do things. Sometimes my mother would break into fits, shouting that I was such an obstacle in her life. My father too said I was a terrible burden. Soon their words turned into beatings.

My mother was very particular about how she kept her house. She would always remind me that if I weren't there it wouldn't be such a mess. Once she started hitting me because she had asked me to make the bed in a particular way. But I had done it another way. "What difference does it make?" I asked.

That made her even angrier. As soon as my father came home she told him that I was disobedient and had the nerve to talk back to her. He took off his belt and started hitting me with it. Then my mother grabbed me by the hair and started slapping me while my father continued with the belt.

Another time I had come into the drawing room not "properly dressed" for company. As soon as the guests left, my mother took a hot spatula from the stove and struck my cheek with it. My skin began to burn. I was so angry I said, "I hate it here, I want to go back."

When my father came in he started striking me with his belt again. "Do you think we want you here?" he asked. "Nobody wants you here. Such an impossible child—but I am going to fix you no matter what. I am going to fix you—I swear." And he kept on hitting me.

At school, my teacher saw the burn mark on my face and asked me what happened. After hesitating I told her. "Your poor mother," she said. "Do you know how much it hurt her to have done this to you? But what else can we do? You children don't learn unless we hit you."

Another girl in the class raised her hand and said, "My mother beats me with a ruler but it's only because she loves me." In India, it was only part of "proper discipline" to hit a child. Over there, it's the parents who never hit their children who are looked upon as neglectful.

Even in school we were beaten. Once, those of us who hadn't done our homework had to stand up and put out our palms so that the teacher could come around and strike us with her ruler. When she got to me she gave me this reproachful look and said, "You see you still haven't learned, you bad girl," and gave me my punishment.

At home, my parents said I was the worst kind of child ever and needed a lot of discipline. "A bad child," they would tell their friends, "so disobedient."

The fact that I was a "bad child" was the answer to everything. My grandparents had sent me back because I was a "bad child." Everyone hated me because I was a bad girl. I started to believe I deserved to be treated this way.

When I was 12, my father was transferred to a job in the U.S. As a teenager in New York City, dealing with my parents became even harder. My friends would go to parties and movies and I would be stuck at home. Sometimes, when I did something they didn't like, my parents wouldn't even let me to go to school.

I wasn't allowed to go out of the house alone until I started going to high school. And even then I had to get home by 4 p.m. One time I went to McDonald's after school to celebrate the birthday of one of my closest friends. I only stayed for about ten minutes, though, because I didn't want to get in trouble. I rushed home and got there by 4:20. My mother was waiting near the door and started slapping me as soon as I walked in.

When my father got home she told him to "ask her which guy was she f--king that she was an hour late." She said I had started to curse at her when she asked for an explanation. I was used to her exaggerating things and didn't even try to defend myself. I knew my father wouldn't wait to hear my side. And he didn't, he just started kicking me and swearing that he would fix me if it took his whole life. I just thought it was my fault. I shouldn't have gone with my friends in the first place.

My friends would invite me to go ice skating and to their parties. My parents would never let me go. After a while I just stopped trying to get permission and the invitations stopped coming. I used to get depressed because I believed no one liked me. My grades started dropping.

Once I tried to join an after-school club. Since it was a writing club I thought that I could just take the work home with me. But when I found out there were meetings I had to attend, I dropped out. I explained to my teacher that I had to get home by four o'clock and that my parents called every day to make sure I was there. "And what would happen if you weren't?" he asked. "I would be in trouble," I answered, trying to say as little as possible.

The teacher wrote my parents a letter asking them to let me join the club but they refused and my father slapped me. He was angry in a way I had never seen him before. How dare I complain to strangers about him?

Although I couldn't imagine telling an adult about what was happening to me, sometimes I would confide in my friends. "You should call the police," some said. But the thought of police coming to our house scared me. "Why don't you run away?" others suggested. Perhaps the worst thing I heard was: "Oh, you're exaggerating, it isn't so bad. Both of your parents are together. You are the only child. What are you complaining about? They're just overprotective."

Then one day, during another conversation with my teacher, I blurted out, "They hit me with a belt." At first I didn't think he was going to take me seriously. I thought he might say something like, "So what? I hit my kids with a belt too." Instead he looked at me very seriously for a moment and then asked, "When was the last time they did that?"

I remembered what my friends had said about calling the police. And I was afraid he was going to do just that. "It's really nothing. I am the one who's bad, really," I said. I was remembering the grade school teacher who had labeled me a "bad child." I hated the way she had embarrassed me in front of the class, but I preferred that to having my parents reported to the police. I tried to explain to him that my parents believed hitting was the best way to discipline a child—that in India hitting a child was considered appropriate, even necessary.

"But with a belt?" my teacher asked. "I have two children; one is 18 and the other is 21. I have never hit them."

I just couldn't believe him. He must have forgotten. I didn't think it was possible to raise kids without ever hitting them.

"Well, you're not going to do anything, are you?" I asked nervously. Inside, I was thinking, "Oh, God, can't you just forget it?"

He explained to me that as a teacher he was required by law to "report" any child he suspected of being abused. The next day I was called to my guidance counselor's office. They told me that they wanted to call my parents.

That night I couldn't sleep. I just couldn't imagine how my parents would react if the school called. The counselor had asked me to describe how I thought my parents would react. All I could manage to say was, "They would be upset." But that was an understatement. I knew the end result would be that they would take me back to India. I wished I could have taken back what I had said.

I tried to figure out how to convince my teacher and counselor that talking to my parents would do more harm than good. Finally they gave me a choice: they wouldn't call my parents if I agreed to go to counseling. Naturally, that's what I chose.

Once a week, I would go to my guidance counselor's office and she'd ask me what happened over the weekend, whether there had been any fights. Of course, it didn't change the situation, but talking about what was happening to me certainly helped me cope with it.

One time I told my counselor how my mother had asked me to iron clothes in a certain order and I had done them in a different order. Before, I had thought I was being disobedient when I didn't do exactly what my parents said. But my counselor made me feel that it was bad enough that I had to iron everyone's clothes. She said that my mother had no right to get upset over the order I did it in.

The counselor made me see that other kids did things that were much worse and yet their parents didn't treat them half as badly as mine treated me. Soon I began to understand that I wasn't responsible for everything and I didn't deserve to be treated that way.

Just talking to my counselor made me feel better. I wondered why I hadn't been able to get to know her before. I guess I had thought that all adults would be like my parents. It was a big relief to find out that it wasn't true.

When summer vacation came I went back to India for a visit. One day I was walking through a park. Some families had built little homes there. One of the women who lived there was slapping a child so hard that I could hear it from down on the corner.

When I got closer I saw a skinny child, about 4 years old, being beaten by his mother. He was naked from head to heels and his skin was red. Tears were rolling down his face but he wasn't shouting. It seemed to me that he was used to this.

Suddenly, on an impulse, I shouted, "Stop it!" The woman looked at me, astounded. "Do you want to kill him?" I asked more calmly.

When the mother finally recovered from the shock of my intrusion, she got very angry. "What's your problem, lady?" she managed to say. "He drank all the milk that we had for the week. Now his father is going to hit me."

She kept shouting angrily at me: "It's none of your business what I do with my children." Just for spite, she struck the kid again. "What are you going to do about it?" she asked.

A good question. What was I going to do about it? Call the Child Welfare Agency? India didn't even have one, as far as I knew. Report the mother to the police? They would probably laugh at me. Get her therapy? Take him home with me when I didn't even have a home of my own?

I looked at the little boy's face again. The tears on his cheeks were almost dry. I turned away and started to leave. "Ha! these rich people think they can control everything," she called after me. "Hey woman, if you love my son so much why don't you take him with you?"

Suddenly I hated myself. Why did I have to butt in if I couldn't do anything in the end? Did parents have eternal control over their children? Why was anyone else powerless to stop them? Why didn't they have a CWA here? And even if they did, would it solve the problem? In the U.S., we still have cases of kids being killed by abusive parents. I realized I had to learn more about child abuse and what to do about it.

When I returned to New York, I decided that no matter what, I was going to help myself and others in my situation. I decided I wanted to do a Westinghouse research project on child abuse. In order to do that I would have to stay at school till 6 p.m. once a week. My parents still expected me home by 4 p.m. every day, but I applied to do the project anyway. I was determined that they weren't going to stop me.

My project proposal was accepted but it was an ordeal to convince my parents to let me do it. It was the new me that they were dealing with, however. I didn't wait for them to give me permission, I just started going. What could they do? Hit me? It seemed like they hit me no matter what I did.

Sometimes my father wouldn't let me in the house when I got home after 6 p.m. Once I had to stay out on the stairs all night. My mother said I was getting out of hand and my father agreed. "We are going to take her back to India as soon as she finishes this damn school," he said. This "American nonsense" was getting to me, they concluded.

One day I came back from school and my father started hitting me with his belt. I was shocked—usually he would at least give a reason before he started beating me.

I thought he had gone crazy. I just looked at him, too stunned to say anything. Then he stopped and said, "This is so that you can do your child abuse report better." Somehow, he had found out what my Westinghouse project was about.

Later my mother grabbed me by the hair and started slapping me. "A report on child abuse," she chuckled. "How daring!" She slapped me again. "How daring!" she repeated. Slap! "Child abuse, hah!" Slap!

Suddenly I couldn't take it anymore. I pushed her away. Before, I would just stand there like a statue and take it when she hit me. But not this time. I left the room and locked myself in the bathroom.

In the bathroom, I cried a little and thought about why they were so upset about my project. I knew other kids who were doing projects on dysfunctional families but their parents didn't get angry with them. It occurred to me for the first time that my parents knew that they were abusing me.

All along I had been thinking that they didn't know any better, that it was just the Indian custom to treat children this way. But they were perfectly aware of what they were doing. No wonder when my teachers spoke to my parents they always came away with the impression that they were just "overprotective." My parents had been treating me this way knowing it was wrong and making sure no one found out.

Suddenly I hated them. I had never felt as angry as I did that day. I used to think that it would be possible for us to have a reconciliation when I got older. But I no longer believe that there is any chance of that.

My parents still talk about taking me back to India to get all the "American crap" out of me. I have other plans, however. I'm going to stay here and study so I can help children like me as much as possible—not just in India, but all over the world. Because no one deserves to be treated the way I have been.

My Terrible Secret:
Breaking the Silence

By Anonymous

The names and a few of the details in this story have been changed.

In my high school creative writing class, we all had to write a short story and read it out loud to our classmates. Jessica, who is 17, got up and began to read her story. At first you couldn't tell what it was about. But when she came to the part about the girl's father telling her to go get her nightgown and to change in front of him, I figured it out. It didn't seem right for a father to watch his daughter undress.

When she finished, the other kids all started talking but I couldn't hear them. It was like they all just disappeared and I sat there staring at nothing at all. The only thing I could see was a naked little girl with two men hovering over her, trying to touch her and telling her how special she was. Then I realized that little girl was me.

Feeling dazed and numb, I couldn't believe that after burying these painful memories for about ten years in my subconscious, they surfaced because of one simple story. I did my best to forget about the images the story had conjured up but something was conspiring against me. Everywhere I turned that day, kids were talking about Jessica's story, wondering if she made it up or if it actually happened to her or someone she knew. They said it seemed too authentic to be fiction. I tried to put up a front as if nothing was wrong. Since none of them knew about my own experience, it was pretty easy. I was surprised that nobody noticed how quiet I was.

The first time it happened I was living in Trinidad, an island in the Caribbean where I was born. I must have been about 7 years old. One night when my mother was at work, her boyfriend came over. He was tall and kind of robust, but I can't really remember his face. He sat in the living room while I was washing dishes in the kitchen.

After I had finished, I went into the living room to watch TV. He came over and lifted me onto his lap and told me he was going to teach me a new game. I didn't think anything of it because he was always lifting me and hugging me. But then he put his hand under my blouse and started feeling my breasts. I remember asking him why Mommy's were so big and mine were so small. (I don't remember his response.)

I asked him what he was doing and he said it was nothing—that big people played this game all the time. Then he started touching me between my legs. I thought it felt icky but he was an adult and to my childish mind, adults were always right; they wouldn't do anything to deliberately hurt a child. I didn't say anything—not even when he put his mouth on mine. I told him I couldn't wait to tell my friends about this new game, but he told me that this was going to be our little secret, that I shouldn't tell anyone else—not even my mommy.

I felt so proud that someone thought I was special enough to teach me a grown-up game. I also felt proud that I could keep a grown-up secret. When I actually thought about what he had done, I felt so confused that I thought maybe I should tell someone. But I didn't.

He continued to see my mother for a while afterwards, but he rarely came inside the house after that. I can't remember if it ever happened again.

When I was around 8 I was living with my godmother and it happened again. In those days, washing machines were very rare in Trinidad so people washed clothes in what we called "bath-tubs," which are big basins with handles.

Well, my godmother only had two small tubs so she would send me to borrow a big one from Mr. Jarvis, this old man who lived across the road. He lived alone because his kids were all grown up. He was skinny and practically all his hair was gone. I had been borrowing his tub for a while and he had never done anything suspicious. But one day when I was returning the tub, he told me to take it inside. Next he told me to wait, that he had a bottle of jam for me. I waited, and somehow between waiting and leaving I found myself flat on my back in this room. (I really can't remember how.) The only thing in there was a big bed and an old chair. The walls weren't even painted.

He started rubbing me and putting his penis all over me. Most people would think it's strange but I didn't do anything. I just laid there and stared at the wall, letting him do what he wanted. He told me that this was just between the two of us—just our se-cret—and that he'd give me anything I wanted.

I didn't know what to do. I felt that something must really be wrong with me. Now two men had done it to me. I couldn't tell my godmother or anyone for that matter. I thought it was my fault—they both did it to me and they didn't even know each other. Since I didn't tell my godmother, I still had to borrow Mr. Jarvis's bathtub. When I had to go, I would have a friend come with me. After my godmother finished washing, I used to go back and drop it in the yard and run away. I was lucky he never got to me again. After I went back to live with my mother, I found out that Mr. Jarvis did the same thing to my godmother's niece and got her pregnant.

I'm now 17, yet the first time I ever told anyone about these two incidents was just four months ago. I told my boyfriend. It was hard at first, but I trusted him and I knew that he wouldn't say anything to put me down. After I told him, he was very quiet. He just held me. That's when I really believed that it wasn't my fault. Here was someone who loved me before he knew and still loved me after he knew. That was the first step toward coming to terms with what happened to me. I am planning to get counseling as soon as I feel I can handle it.

To this day, there are still men who try to touch me where they shouldn't. But now I am older and I have confidence and pride in myself. That's what you need to face the world without letting some man "cop a feel."

For those people who may have been sexually abused, it's not your fault. You must not keep it a secret no matter how long ago it happened. It won't go away by itself. Tell someone. It's a heavy burden to carry alone.

No One Spoke Up for Irma

By Ana Angélica Pines

The names in this story have been changed.

They say if you look into someone's eyes you can see her soul. When I look into my friend Irma's eyes, I see reflections of the past. We're around 5 or 6 years old and we're crossing the street on the way to the fruit market. Suddenly the cart that Irma's mother, Carmen, is pushing tips over and her groceries fall out in the middle of the street. She grabs Irma's head and bangs it against the handbar of the cart. Irma is bleeding from her lip now and both she and her younger sister Lydia are crying as we all help pick the stuff up off the ground.

The next thing I know my mother, my sister, and I are walking away as if nothing has happened. Lydia comes running after us and grabs onto my mother's leg. "Don't let her hit me!" she screams. Carmen comes over, takes Lydia by the arm, and pulls her back across the street to where Irma is standing, still in tears. As we walk away nobody says a word. To this day I still don't know what to think about that moment.

Irma is 16 now. The two of us grew up together, and ever since we were little Irma's mother would hit her, throw things at her, call her a "b--ch," and tell her to "go wash [her] dirty ass." She would buy Lydia things and take her places but she always ignored Irma and made her stay behind.

Everyone on the block saw what was going on, but no one ever did anything to stop it. As far as I could see, the kids were the only ones who ever confronted Carmen about what she was doing. We quickly got the message, however, that if we kept it up we'd get in trouble. As long as they kept us quiet, the adults could pretend the problem didn't exist.

For some reason, Carmen always favored Lydia over Irma. They could do the same things but only Irma would get in trouble. When Irma turned 5, for example, there was a joint birthday party for her and her older brother. Lydia didn't want food, she wanted candy, so she threw her food away. Irma saw this and did the same. Carmen grabbed Irma and slapped her right in front of everybody (and on her birthday). Then she forced her to eat all the food on her plate (an illogical amount to give a little girl in the first place). My sister fed it to her while wiping her tears and we put some on my plate when Carmen wasn't looking.

Carmen's abuse wasn't always physical, however. On Christmas morning her siblings would still be opening their presents half an hour after Irma had finished. Every fall she and her sister would get jeans and some shirts to start off the school year. But as the year progressed, Lydia's wardrobe would continue to grow, while Irma's stayed the same. All through junior high school she wore the same thing every week. Irma was never allowed to go out either. Anytime we asked if she could go someplace with us we were told that she was being punished or that she just couldn't go.

Once when we were around 7 or 8, Peter, one of the kids from the block, had the guts to go up to Carmen and ask her, "Why can Lydia come downstairs and not Irma?" Not long after that, a girl named Melissa decided to go up to Carmen and tell her to her face: "You're a child abuser!" Carmen got really mad and I remember thinking to myself, "She knows she is." When they heard about what happened, both Pete's mother and Melissa's told them the same thing: "Mind your own business."

After I was around 7 or 8 I hardly ever went to Irma and Lydia's house; I couldn't stand to watch it anymore. But my sister was always over there—she was practically a member of the family. Irma always had to fold everybody's laundry, sweep and mop and basically clean the whole house, and when Carmen wasn't there, my sister would help her.

Other times, my sister would grab Carmen when she was about to hit Irma and take her outside for a walk to calm her down. I often wonder how many more beatings Irma would have gotten if it hadn't been for my sister. But most of the neighbors just accepted the situation. In fact they used to favor Lydia just as much as Carmen did. They'd give her better presents on Christmas and take her to the beach and upstate to the Seven Lakes in the summertime while Irma always had to stay at home. At times my family took Lydia places too. After all it wasn't her fault. She was just a child herself.

Two summers ago Lydia got to go visit relatives in Florida and once again Irma was going to have to stay home. My family was going to Guatemala and my mother offered to take her with us.

"I'm not giving her anything," said Carmen.

"Fine, I'll pay for everything," my mother told her. But we ended up not taking her because it was too late to get Irma a passport.

When Irma turned 16 last year her mother wasn't planning to do anything for her—not even dinner. So my family decided to throw her our own surprise party at my cousin's house. We had *pernil, arroz con gandules,* a big cake. There were *kapias* and *recuerdos* (little ceramic figurines) for people to take home and we took lots of pictures. The funny thing was that Irma didn't even know half the people there. Nobody from her family came. When we told Carmen she said, "No one from this house is going."

Since the people at the party knew about Irma's situation they all chipped in and even bought her gifts. It was awkward, but

Irma enjoyed it. When Carmen found out, however, she got mad and started crying. Lydia always had piñatas, candy, and presents on her birthday, and when she turns 16 next year Carmen is planning to have a big ceremony with the *damas* and *caballeros* (girls in fancy dresses, guys in tuxedos) and everything. But for some reason Carmen doesn't want Irma to have anything in life.

About a year ago, my mother offered to adopt Irma. She told Carmen that if she didn't want her, Irma could come live with us. But Carmen made excuses, saying Irma was lazy and stupid and that she didn't want us to have to put up with what she had. When she saw that my mother was serious she just told her "no" and walked out.

When somebody tells you something enough times, sooner or later you begin to believe it. For example, back when we were younger, Lydia, many of the other girls on the block, and I all used to go to dancing school while Irma stayed home and did chores. Her mother's excuse was that Irma wasn't any good at dance and didn't like it. She repeated it so many times that Irma eventually agreed with her.

Irma's family always told her that she was worthless too, that she'd never do anything in life but get married, have kids, and cook eggs all day. She says worthless is how she now feels and "that's what they expect so that's what I'm going to give them." Lately Irma's been doing very badly in school; she cuts all the time and failed every class but one last semester. She gets into fights a lot and always wears baggy jeans and the same shirt that she bought at Warner Brothers with money that her father gave her. She hardly ever wears makeup and she talks like a hoodlum.

A couple of years ago she was in the hospital and she told my sister that she wished she had died so she would never have had to go back to that house again. I try to make things appealing to her so she'll want to do better. "If you're sick of your house go to school," I tell her. "Then you can graduate on time and move out, go to college, or get a job. You can even move in with me."

It's strange, even though Irma grew up with nothing she still turned out to be so superficial and ditzy. She's only interested in name-brand clothing and if she gets any money she blows it on sneakers. These days Irma always has this blank look on her face—like there's nothing there. It's like looking into space. It's scary. She's so lost and seems to have no sense of direction.

In June, my sister and I were on the train with Irma and noticed she had carved her name in her arm with a needle. We asked her why and she just said it was because she wanted to feel pain. I guess pain is what she's used to feeling. I don't know. I don't understand how she thinks. Sometimes I can't help but ask myself, "Why is she so stupid?" but then I think about the way she's always been told how worthless she is.

Don't get me wrong, Irma has a lot of friends and people like her, but what good are friends if you don't like yourself? Sometimes I wish I could just hold her and tell her that everything is going to be okay. I wish I could predict the future but I can't. The only thing that can be done now is for her to get help.

So many people have seen the pain Irma suffered and stayed quiet. Everyone on the block knows what's been going on. We all did little things to make Irma feel better but no one ever really spoke up or tried to get her out of the situation. When I was little I thought a lot about calling those hotlines for abused children, but I was always afraid they would somehow be able to figure out who I was. I thought maybe they'd blow me off because I was only a child and then not do anything anyway. Not many of the adults I knew listened to children.

But what if they did show up at the house? On the news you always hear about kids being beaten even after they were visited by social workers. Carmen probably would have thought Irma had been the one who called and beaten her more severely to keep her quiet. I never trusted anyone. That's why I didn't call. It seemed like it would have just made the situation worse. Why should the adults at the hotlines be any different from the ones on my block? If the people who knew Irma didn't do anything to help her, then what reason did I have to think that total strangers would?

When something like this is happening around us and we keep

silent, then we're all to blame—including me. People always say "mind your business," but when it's happening right upstairs or down the hall and you're a witness, it becomes part of your life as well. In other words, it is your business.

Silence isn't always golden. Sometimes silence is pain.

A Proud Moment: Reporting the Abuse Upstairs

By Jessica Cabassa

When I lived in Brooklyn, I lived near a family who kept hitting their child. I mean every day. The little girl was 10 years old. She had to clean and do the wash, and only got to eat scraps and leftovers. My aunt and I visited the family to talk to them. The girl was a mess.

She used to come down to ask us for butter and stuff. My mom always gave. One time she went to my room and started talking to me about how her mother was sick and her stepfather would get drunk and start hitting her.

I felt sorry for the girl, and told my mother how she was neglected and mistreated. My mother said, "Leave it alone." But I was too scared and just couldn't get it out of my mind. The girl attended my sister's school. What could I do? Stay home and act like the screaming was just a movie?

The next day the girl came down to ask for bread. She was all bruised up and had old-lady powder on to try to cover it up. I knew this wasn't my business, but what can I say? It had to stop. The next day I called the cops and reported the child abuse.

When the cops came to my house, they asked me questions such as "Does she get hit every day?" I said, "Yes." My mother backed me up. They took the stepfather and arrested him. They treated the mother and put the girl in a foster home.

The girl is now in a foster home where she is treated nicely. She thanked me for what I did, and we have continued to write to each other. I will always be proud of what I did.

The Mind Slowly Begins to Defrost

Loss

Will There Ever Be Justice for David?

By Grismaldy Laboy

Spray-painted on a wall at the corner of 153rd Street and Morris Avenue in the South Bronx in big multicolored letters is the name Dave and the words "We Love You." It is a curbside shrine to my cousin, David Elias Torres, who two years ago was shot in cold blood while talking to his girlfriend on the pay phone across the street. Eight blocks uptown sits the Bronx Supreme Courthouse where the man who was charged with David's murder was tried, found not guilty, and released.

David was 20 when he was killed. His life ended before it ever really began. He grew up in a three-bedroom apartment on the third floor of an apartment complex across the street from his mural with his mother and brothers, José and Héctor. The neighborhood around there was full of hoodlums hanging out in front of the building or chilling on the corner.

When we were little, David was always curious. I remember

him trying to get us all to come with him across an abandoned bridge near where he lived so we could see the trains pass by. As he got older, David let his curiosity get him into trouble. By the time he was 15, he was hanging out with people who dealt drugs and staying out late at night partying. At 16, he dropped out of school, and three years later he was arrested in an apartment containing drugs and guns and charged with possession of weapons and narcotics. He was sentenced to twenty years in jail but was released on parole after eleven months when he agreed to give the police some information they wanted.

I hadn't seen David in over a year and I missed him. So two weeks after he got out, on a Saturday, I took the bus over to see him. When I got there, he was cleaning his room, throwing out some of his jeans, shirts, jackets, sneakers, some pictures and magazines. He had pumped a lot of iron in prison and showed off his muscles to me. His mother, Titi Ana, was scolding David, "*Mira, muchacho, no 'te' botando todo, que no hay dinero para comprar má'.*" (Don't be throwing out everything; we don't have money to replace it.)

"*Ay, no te apures, Mami. Yo voy a conseguir un trabajo,*" David said, smiling. (Don't worry, Mom. I'm going to get a job.)

He said he had an interview that Tuesday at the Big Apple Messenger Service in Manhattan. David seemed determined to change his life around. In jail, he had taken classes toward his GED and now he spoke proudly about going to night school to finish. As we talked, he rearranged the furniture in his room, trying to give it a new look. He said he wanted a new start. He wanted to put his mistakes behind him and was throwing away anything and everything that reminded him of his past. "I should have done this a long time ago," he said.

My fifteenth birthday was only two weeks away and he kept giving me weird suggestions on what to do to celebrate. Like he told me to walk around all of Manhattan with my friends in the freezing cold. I looked at him like he was crazy. We joked around some more and then I gave him a hug and a kiss and said good-bye. "God bless!" he said.

Three days later, I was chilling at home with my older brother, José Elias, who was home from college on vacation. We were watching TV and catching up on each other's lives, when the phone rang. It was Nirma, a friend of the family who lived downstairs from David. Nirma never called us, so immediately I knew something was up.

"I don't know how to say this. . . . David's been shot," she told me.

"What?" I yelled into the phone as a chill ran through my entire body.

"David's been shot."

José snatched the phone from my hand and talked to Nirma for what seemed like an eternity. Then he hung up and stared into my eyes.

"David's been shot," José told me, on the brink of tears.

"Is he okay?" I asked, already knowing the answer in my heart.

"He's dead." The words echoed throughout the house and I looked away in disbelief.

He said Nirma had heard shots fired and a lot of commotion so she ran outside to see what happened. There was David lying on the ground across the street, bleeding from his head. The ambulance had come, but there was no need for it. David was dead.

Somehow, José's words didn't sink in. I remained standing. I felt numb. I wasn't quite sure what was happening. Maybe I had misunderstood or maybe José had.

José zoomed out of his pj's and got dressed fast. I didn't know what to do. I didn't know what to think. I just stood there for a long time waiting for someone to tell me, "This is only a bad dream. It's not real."

"I'm leaving to go see what happened," José told me. "Call Ma and Pa at work to tell them what happened."

After the door closed, I just sat there on the sofa alone, stunned, tears rolling down my cheeks. I was too scared to call my parents, scared of the truth. "It's not true," I kept telling myself. "It's not true."

Finally, I got myself together and called my father. I didn't know how to tell him so I just blurted out, "David got shot."

My father sighed and said, "Oh my God, how is he?"

"He's dead."

"Are you sure he's dead?" he kept asking me.

"Yes," I remember saying. "David's dead!" Only when I said it out loud did I believe it was really true.

My mother was already on her way home from work and as soon as both she and my father arrived, we went straight over to David's house.

It was true. There were bloodstains on the concrete in front of the bodega. Yellow police tape surrounded the crime scene and most of my relatives were looking on in disbelief.

The next day, Wednesday, there was a picture in the *Daily News* of the store owners washing away the bloodstains on the sidewalk underneath the pay phone. In a brief two sentences under the picture, it said that an unidentified Hispanic male in his early twenties was killed outside a store in the South Bronx. It might as well have just said, "Oh, by the way, some nobody was killed in—where else?—the South Bronx."

I felt horrible. I'd seen in the news how teenagers in New York City were dying left and right, but I never figured it would hit so close to home. David was family, my blood. Reality is hard to swallow sometimes, and this was one of those times for me.

The day after that, Thursday, was the wake. A part of me didn't want to go. I wanted to remember David as I last saw him. But I went anyway. The funeral home was packed and everyone was crying—some hysterically, others quietly. "*¡Dios, mi hijo! Me cogieron mi hijo,*" Titi Ana kept yelling. "God, my son! They took my son!"

David left a lot of people behind. His younger brother, Héctor, for example, who always looked up to him. Héctor had heard the shots, ran to where David lay on the ground, and sat in the pool of blood holding David's head on his lap. At 15, it was a hard blow to withstand.

On the final day of the wake, before they closed the casket, everyone lined up to see David one final time. When it was my turn, I looked at David's face. I could see the marks where the bullet had pierced his head. I kissed him on the forehead one final time. He was so cold that I started to cry.

Once David had been lowered into his grave questions began to pop up about who killed him and why. Who witnessed it? Rumors began to spread. Everyone had a different story. Some said Johnny A., a kid from the neighborhood who grew up with David and had a reputation as a troublemaker, got out of an "O.J. car," came toward David, shot him in the head, got back in the car, and drove off. Others claimed there was someone else driving the car and Johnny didn't act alone. But all the stories we heard from people in the neighborhood agreed that Johnny was the one who pulled the trigger.

After David was buried, the whole family came together every day to pray for him and say a rosary. That's where David's girlfriend, Marisol, told us that the day he died, David passed by her job at Lincoln Hospital to get her keys. On his way home, which was only two blocks away from the hospital, David called her and told her that he had seen Johnny A. and Johnny appeared to be stalking him in a car. "I think he's going to kill me," he told her. They continued talking until Marisol heard shots through the phone and ran out of the hospital and down two blocks to where David lay dead on the ground.

My cousin José told me that two days after the shooting, Johnny, knowing the police were looking for him, went to the 41st Precinct and turned himself in. He was arrested and charged with second-degree murder. José said that Johnny had confessed.

José also said that he heard that another kid from the block, George Rivera, 15, was coming out of the video store and saw Johnny drive up in an "O.J. car," get out, approach David, and shoot him in the head twice at close range. Then he got back in his car and drove off. That's what Rivera told the police.

According to José, David's neighbors Shiree and Irma, the ones who first called the police, also witnessed the shooting out their living room window and said it was Johnny. In short,

everything pointed to Johnny, and after he was arrested, he went
to jail to await trial.

It eased our suffering to believe that the person who did this
to David was locked up and had no chance to roam the streets
and possibly kill again. The prosecutor appointed to the case informed the family that the chances of convicting Johnny were
very good. We had the witnesses and the confession. We were
confident that the justice system would make Johnny pay for
what he had done by locking him up for a long time.

Two very slow years passed while we waited for the trial to
begin. When it did, last May, things quickly started to go wrong.
Some of the witnesses changed their stories about what they had
seen. Rumor had it they were either scared or that someone paid
them off to keep their mouths shut or change their testimony.

When the time came for Johnny himself to testify, I went to
court. Johnny claimed that the police forced the confession out
of him. He described how he was handcuffed to a pole by his left
wrist and how, as they were questioning him, they kept moving
him farther and farther from the pole until his arm was completely stretched out. His defense lawyer, who had his hair
slicked back like Pat Riley, showed pictures of Johnny looking
fine upon arrival at the police station but with many bruises on
his face later.

I wanted to throw up. Johnny was acting like he was the victim. He kept whining and whining about how bad the police
treated him and looking more innocent all the time. I could tell
the jury felt bad for Johnny. (Well, the jurors who were awake
anyway, because one old lady was knocked out.) They had that
"*¡Ay, bendito!*" look on their faces.

Then Johnny's lawyer asked him to describe his friendship
with David. Johnny told the court how much he loved David,
how he missed him, and how he could never have done what
they said. As he kept talking, it was like a knife was being stuck
into my heart, piercing it again and again until I almost died. I
couldn't believe what I was witnessing.

When it was the prosecutor's turn, he seemed to be doing a

horrible job. When he had Johnny on the stand during cross-examination, I thought he made him look better instead of worse. Johnny's wife had claimed he was with her at the time of the shooting. They went through this whole thing about the exact time and she said she was sure because they had been listening to the radio. But in his testimony, Johnny mentioned that it was a tape they were listening to. I felt the prosecutor should have pinned Johnny into a corner and called attention to the inconsistencies in their testimonies, but he didn't.

After the jury had left the courtroom, the judge insulted the prosecutor on his lazy and unorganized style and told him to get his act together and stop complaining about his rulings. When I heard that, I knew it wasn't just my emotions getting the best of me. If a judge—who knows a lot more about law than I do—noticed how poorly the prosecutor was doing, then something was very wrong in this trial after all. And the prosecutor wasn't the only thing wrong with the trial. While witnesses were testifying, the jury seemed uninterested, in another world. You could tell by the bored looks on their faces that they weren't focusing, that they just wanted to get this case over with. I felt the walls closing in on the whole case and in the pit of my stomach I began to fear that Johnny would be set free.

But I swallowed my fear, telling myself to believe in justice. The system would not allow a killer to roam the streets. The weekend passed and it took a couple more days for the closing arguments and other procedural matters. It was finals week at school and I tried to focus on my exams, but it was difficult. Then one day, I got home from school and my mom, who's usually chipper and eager to tell me about her day, was sitting on the sofa with a dim look on her face.

"What's wrong? What happened?" I asked.

"They let him go," she responded.

"They let who go?" I asked, although I already knew the answer.

"Johnny."

What I felt at that moment was beyond hurt and beyond

anger. I felt rage. It brought me back to the day David died. I felt like he had been killed a second time, by the justice system. Now everything had been taken from us. We had no David. We had no justice.

The day of the verdict, the family gathered together in Titi Ana's house. We looked at old pictures of David and cried, remembering how things used to be.

The prosecutor told my cousin José that he was sorry. He had tried his best and there was nothing more that could be done. No one told us that Johnny could still be sued in civil court on wrongful death charges.

Later on that day, we all went to the cemetery. Titi Ana collapsed on top of David's grave, crying hysterically. "*Quiero mi hijo*," she screamed. "*Dios, por favor, dame mi hijo.*" (I want my son. Please, God, give me my son.) David's brother, Héctor, now 17, had an expressionless look on his face that remained there for weeks following the verdict.

It all seemed so hopeless. It was the emptiest feeling I have ever experienced and it continues to this day. The jury's verdict was final. To them, it is over and done with. But to us, it will never be over.

It's not supposed to work this way. I was taught that if you kill, you go to jail. You pay for yanking a loved one out of a family's life. But no one has paid for David's murder. His killer is free to roam the streets while David lies six feet under. Even though Johnny was acquitted, and we could never prove he killed David, I still feel in my heart he was responsible. A month after he was released from jail, I was walking down Southern Boulevard to the bus when I saw Johnny coming the other way. He didn't know who I was, but I recognized him from the trial. I stopped walking, stood near a store, and watched him as he strolled right by me.

He was wearing a nice dark suit and had his head held high like he was on top of the world. So many things ran through my mind at that moment. I felt like confronting him and spitting in his face. I wished he could feel what I felt when David was buried. I wished he had seen Titi Ana when she collapsed on David's grave wanting her son back. I wished he could feel what we were all going through and realize how much David meant to us.

My first thought was that Johnny should die. He seemed to have no remorse. I was convinced that what my family and I had gone through meant absolutely nothing to him and I wanted him to suffer like we suffered. I wanted him to pay. I felt like doing so many things, but I kept my cool and refused to let my emotions get the best of me. I didn't want to lower myself to his level.

They say there is no justice in this world, but I don't believe that. One way or another, the person who killed David will get what he deserves. If this world doesn't provide its justice, then I leave it up to God to provide his. David's murderer may have escaped the justice system, but sooner or later, what he did will catch up to him.

Maribel Feliciano: She Died in the Arms of a Friend

By Adrian Jefferson

Can you imagine your best friend dying in your arms? That's what happened to Yvette. Her best friend, Maribel Feliciano, was stabbed to death on the subway when the two girls were on their way home from school. When I asked Yvette to tell me about what happened, she sounded sad, but also very calm and strong. This is her story.

On September 18, Yvette and Maribel, both 15 and students at the High School of Fashion Industries, were on the C train on their way home to Sheridan Avenue, East New York. They always rode this train home from school together without any problems. But that day they didn't feel comfortable, they felt something wasn't right. "We were about to get off the train because we were the only Hispanic girls," Yvette said. Then, before the train got to the next stop, four girls surrounded them. Yvette says that one of them threatened Maribel, saying, "You'd better run or we're gonna stab you."

Maribel didn't want to appear to be a coward or look like a sucker so she said she wouldn't run. The girl who had threatened her hit Maribel in the face twice. Yvette, in defense of her friend, hit the girl back. The girl pushed Yvette down on the floor. "That's when the other girls pulled Maribel down by her hair and one of the girls stabbed her," said Yvette. "I tried to help Maribel by grabbing her hand, but Maribel let go of it and fell. I ran for the conductor and when I got back Maribel was on the floor spitting up blood."

A man took off his shirt and gave it to Yvette. She used it to put pressure on Maribel's back to try to stop the bleeding. At the precinct, the police broke the news to Yvette that Maribel was dead. But Yvette says she already knew. "I remember when I was younger and I asked my mother why, in the movies, people spat up blood and she said it meant they were dead. That's how I knew Maribel was dead," she told me.

Yvette says that she was asked to identify the knife that the police found on the subway tracks. She was also asked to pick the girls who attacked Maribel out of a line-up, which she did. Two were 14, the others were 15 and 16. Yvette said the 15-year-old was the one who stabbed Maribel.

The media said that the girls wanted to rob Maribel for her earrings but Yvette told me that's not what happened. "I don't know why they started with her. I heard a rumor that four guys dared the girls to start with us," she said.

Yvette said she'll never be able to forgive the girls who killed her friend. "They knew what they were doing, there wasn't no remorse," she said.

Although Yvette wasn't hurt physically, this whole experience has been very traumatic for her. She says she was afraid to go to school after it happened. "I was scared, I felt angry too, and I felt very upset," Yvette said. Her mother is also scared and rides the train to school with Yvette every morning.

Yvette thought that people would be understanding about what happened but she discovered that many people had it in for her. She told me that some of the people at Maribel's wake and funeral wanted to jump her because they thought she had run off and left Maribel instead of helping her. But Yvette said that Maribel's family stood by her, saying, "We'd rather our daughter die in the arms of a friend than an enemy."

Yvette also heard a rumor that 200 kids who knew the girls who attacked Maribel wanted to come and finish her off too.

Yvette says that things have cooled off a lot, but she still hasn't gotten over Maribel's death. She gets therapy every Friday and she has supportive family members who do whatever they can to help. "They don't leave me alone," Yvette said. "When I'm alone I think about Maribel and I get depressed."

Yvette said that she thinks about Maribel all the time. "Maribel was very funny, very short, and she had a Miss Piggy nose," Yvette recalled jokingly. "She wouldn't give up nothing without a fight." Yvette remembered how Maribel used to come pick her up in the morning. "My mother makes pancakes every morning and before we left for school we'd split the pancakes." So now, every day at breakfast, Yvette remembers her friend. "Everything I do reminds me of her," she said.

Yvette has met a lot of people because of what happened but she believes nobody can take Maribel's place. "She was my best friend and only friend, nobody can replace her."

His Sneakers, My Dreams

By Suzanne Joblonski

My criminal justice class last spring was really boring. I was always tired because it was my last class of the day. When the teacher talked about the difference between first- and second-degree murder, I would drift into dreamland. I would imagine what my future might be like, think of another idea for a story or poem, or of what my boyfriend and I would be doing that weekend.

Sometimes, I would stare at the sneakers of the guy who sat next to me. He had two pair—one black, one white. Ballys, I think. I always wondered where he'd been in them, the kinds of places he went.

I'll call him Sam. He was the first person I spoke to on the first day of class. When class was over, I noticed he had forgotten his umbrella underneath his chair and I told him. He thanked me and smiled. That was the only time I ever really spoke to Sam, even though I sat next to him five days a week. I also remember he and another girl in class were always annoying one another, and the teacher used to joke that they'd end up getting married.

At the beginning of the term, the teacher asked us to talk about ourselves and our future plans. Most of us had some kind of long-term plan. One girl wanted to be a lawyer, another a social worker, and one of the guys wanted to be a cop. Right after graduation, Sam said, he was going to go into the military. After that he wanted to become a corrections officer.

Last May (I remember it as if it were five minutes ago), I was sitting in my auto shop class. The teacher looked really upset and somebody asked him what was the matter. He told us that one of his students had been shot and killed over the weekend. He mentioned the name, which sounded familiar to me. Wasn't that the guy who sat next to me in my criminal justice class? The only way I could be sure was to see if he was sitting in his usual seat that afternoon. He was always there and always on time.

When I went to class, the seat was empty and everyone had tears in their eyes. My teacher broke the news to us: Sam was the student killed over the weekend. It was over something stupid— I think he stepped on someone's sneakers and they got into an argument. He was killed just two weeks after we learned about the different charges for murder.

I don't usually cry a lot, but this time I did. I cried because he was a teenager and I was a teenager. My tears were for the loss of one of our own. It was as bad as if he were a member of my own family. I am really scared that this won't be the last time this will happen to someone I know. It's been happening every day to my peers around the city. Teenagers are losing friends over stupid things—dirty looks, clothes, jealousy, and revenge.

I have one message for Sam's killers and for teenagers around New York City. Even if it looks hopeless, we are our world's future. Maybe if you plan ahead, you too can have something to look forward to. I know Sam did and so do I.

Remembering Mike

By Carlos Lavezzari

It was the winter of 1990, very close to Christmas. I remember coming home from a friend's house about 3:30 in the afternoon and seeing two Channel 7 news vans parked in front of my building. There were people all over the place in a frantic state. Some of my friends and neighbors were standing around, crying.

I ran up to try to get someone to tell me what had happened. No one answered me so I went inside. In the lobby all of the holiday decorations were ripped down and the Christmas tree looked as if it had been trampled. Just then one of my friends came downstairs saying that Mike had been shot.

I couldn't believe it. I had just played basketball with Mike the day before and he was saying how one day he was going to play for the NBA. And now he was dead?

I ran outside to see if it was true. I saw Mike's sister with a look on her face as if she were lost. One of my friends walked up to me and told me the first of many stories I was to hear about what had happened. He said Mike had been in a schoolyard with a Puerto Rican girl whose brother was the local gang's leader. Mike was sitting with the girl, eating. Three members of the gang walked up and told them that they were going to tell her brother.

When the girl's brother got there he said, "I don't want my sister round no n--gers," and shot everyone in the park. He caught one of my friends in the leg, another in the arm, and Mike in the chest.

After hearing this I found myself wishing I had been there, thinking maybe I could have done something. Maybe I could have talked him into going home or been able to warn him about the type of person the girl's brother was. I started feeling bad, bad about the fact that I never told him how thankful I was for all the times he had my back in a fight, or for letting me hide in his house at times when people wanted to jump me. I never got to thank him for sneaking me into his house when I ran away from home, or for being a good friend to talk to when I was feeling down.

The last thing I remember saying to him was, "See you tomorrow." "Tomorrow" was the day he died.

Now I see how life is taken for granted. Youth today are known to do that. You think because you're young you have many days to look forward to. You've got time to burn. But that may not be true, as I have learned. If anything, this tragic incident taught me two lessons: never take people important to you for granted and never wait to tell someone just how much they mean to you. You never know when it will be your last time seeing them.

No One Deserves to Die Like That

By Wunika Hicks

Damn. Another Black man is gunned down like a wild animal and all around me, people are coming up with their own conclusions about why he got killed. Biggie Smalls is murdered just six months after Tupac and instead of reaching out to each other in sorrow or coming together to make a change, it seems like everyone just wants to point a finger. Some say his death had to do with that East Coast/West Coast thing, while others say he lived a violent life and died the same way.

Now, maybe that's true and maybe it isn't. I didn't know the man personally so I couldn't tell you. But what I will tell you is that it disgusts me to hear people trying to justify his death because of the life he *may have* led. I'm sure Biggie wasn't a saint, but it doesn't matter. No one deserves to die like that.

I keep thinking about how Biggie's children are going to feel. When your father is murdered, do you really care who did it or why? The answer is no.

When I was two years old, I saw my father laying in the street, shot dead. My family didn't know who killed him, they just knew that they had to make some funeral arrangements.

I still feel the pain of that loss. That's why I find it so hard to hear people talk about Biggie's murder, as if maybe he did something to deserve it.

After my pops passed away, nothing was ever the same for us. My mother had two nervous breakdowns, and I lived with relatives. When Mommy got better, I went back to live with her. She went on welfare and we moved out of our house and into the projects. And in order to survive when those little checks ran out, we would go out into the night (my moms had her gun at her side) and hunt for five-cent refund bottles. And when that wasn't enough my mother slept with men for money so we could eat.

That's why I related to Biggie and Tupac. My childhood wasn't the best and neither were theirs. I understood when Biggie was rapping about winter nights with no heat, Christmases and birthdays that passed him by. I went through it myself. I felt it inside. And when Tupac sang about his mother scraping to help him and his sister eat, I related to that too. I also related to the world of guns and drugs they described in their songs because I grew up in it.

A lot of people criticized Biggie and Tupac for portraying a life of violence, guns, and drugs in their music and being a bad influence on the youth who listened to them. Now, I agree that drugs and violence are bad things but I don't think it's fair to blame rap music for the fact that they exist. Violence and drugs were here before rap existed and before Biggie and Tupac were born—right along with teen pregnancy, welfare, and fatherless homes.

The good thing about rap music is that it lets people who have never set foot in the ghetto see what is going on. It lets them know what life is like for those of us not lucky enough to be born in the suburbs with silver spoons in our mouths. How it's a struggle to survive when the school system sucks and a job isn't the easiest thing to find. Instead of blaming rap music, how about blaming the government for allowing people to become poor and homeless and for making children's educations less of a priority than building new jail cells?

We also have to take responsibility for our own actions. Although many of us are under a lot of pressure to sell and use drugs, a strong positive person will ignore it. We can set goals for ourselves—like going to school and getting a diploma, even though some of our teachers are full of crap. And taking a job that only pays $4.75 an hour because it's better than nothing.

Regardless of how you were raised or the bad situations you may find yourself in, you have to be responsible for you. At some point in your life, you have to choose to do something positive with your life. I believe that's what Tupac and Biggie did when they started to rap about some of the wrongs in our society that were being ignored. It's just sad that they had to die by the same bullets they rapped about.

Tupac and Biggie are just a couple of new names to add to a long list of vicious deaths. It doesn't matter who killed them or why. What matters is that they're gone and they won't be the last unless a lot of things change. I'm just thankful that they let me feel their verses and beats. They showed me that people can come up from the ghetto and not just make it, but make it and still relate to those who are still living with the poverty and violence. Now maybe their music didn't solve all our problems but, to tell the truth, I didn't expect it to.

It was enough for me to just enjoy their music and admire their talent. They may not have been perfect but that's because they were human, just like the rest of us. Like my man Biggie would say: "It's all good baby, baby."

How I Made Peace
with the Past

By Paula M. Verma

I remember the sadness in my mother's eyes as we sat in her hospital room, watching her deteriorate as the days went by. My mother had AIDS, the disease that affects your immune system, and she had been in and out of the hospital for months. After she was hospitalized last January and had to have an operation, my youngest brother, Tyrone, and I weren't allowed to go see her at first. But as soon as she was able to speak, we went to visit. As we were coming to my mother's room, all of a sudden my heart started beating real heavy. I thought it was going to stop right there. I was so scared because I didn't know what to expect.

I had heard from my oldest brother, William, that she was getting worse, but when I got close to the bed I couldn't believe that the small woman lying there was my mother. She had lost way too much weight. I wanted to hug her but was too afraid of hurting her, so I didn't. I just said hello, tears rolling down my face.

You could hear in her voice that she was very sick and weak. It seemed as if she knew her time was coming.

She had gotten so sick that she wasn't able to move or get out of bed. She couldn't use the bathroom, so they had put Pampers on her. I did not like the sight of my mother laying in bed powerless, unable to function. I tried to have a conversation with her.

"Hi, Ma. Are you all right? Is the hospital treating you good? Are you eating all your food?" (She didn't like the hospital foods, so my brother brought her something else whenever he could.)

But her only reply was, "Yes ma'am." From that day forward, our names became "ma'am." You see, while my mother was in the hospital, the doctors found out she had dementia, a deterioration or loss of mental faculties. It's similar to Alzheimer's disease that older people get.

While my brother William was explaining her sickness to me and Tyrone, a tall lady entered the room. She introduced herself as Ms. Cynthia Allen, my mother's social worker. She started telling me and my brothers how important it was that we come as often as we could, because they didn't know when my mother was going to leave this earth.

I wanted to scream as loud as I could to get out all the anger I was feeling. I felt so confused. I tried to picture life without my mother, and I knew it would be hard because it would mean I wouldn't have a mother or a father.

I had lost my father to AIDS and drugs also, seven years earlier. Our mother was all we had now, and soon we would have to give her up, too. It was just too much to take in. I remembered all those times I would cry myself to sleep, because I missed her very much, and I knew she was going to die. But I always thought that the people who did the research on AIDS would soon find a cure.

It was hurtful to know that soon she would no longer be there for me, because we were just beginning to build up our relationship again. Me and my brothers had to grow up fast for our ages.

(I'm 18, Tyrone is 17, and William is 20.) We also have a new addition to our family who's 5 years old and is also suffering from AIDS. She was infected in the womb because my mother had unprotected sex. When my mother first found out that my sister had the disease, she gave her up for adoption. My sister is well aware of her sickness, she's very healthy, and she takes her own medication daily.

There was a time when I was so mad at my mother for not being there for us that I stopped going on home visits and kept myself isolated from her. I was very bitter that she transmitted AIDS to my sister. I kept remembering how she used to always tell me how important it was to never have sex without a condom, because you could be at risk. Then she went and did the opposite.

But after she went in the hospital in January, my ways of thinking started to change. I had to learn to forgive her mistakes and accept what happened to my mother and my sister. It was a terrible accident that my mother wouldn't have made had she not been taken over by drugs. A one-night stand for money cost my mother her kids, her health, and even her life. But what was done was done. I had to overcome all that and learn to communicate with her. After all, she was still my mother, no matter what.

So I slowly began to build up a relationship with her. However, my first step in doing that was to let her know how she hurt me. I had to express my anger and how I felt to her for the first time. My mother did the one thing that no child should ever have to face. She chose her boyfriend over her own children. I explained to her that she was wrong because she was my mother, and no man should come between us. Her only reply was that she was sorry for everything she did. I also told her that I hated all of her stealing and lying for money. I told her she should have been there for her children. A mother is supposed to help you, not hurt you.

She told me if she could take everything back she would, but she couldn't. She said she was truly sorry that she let her children down, but she would like to own up to her mistakes. I told her that I knew she was sorry, but I couldn't hold in my anger toward her anymore. Expressing my feelings toward her enabled me to have faith in my mother again.

I will never forget, one day I went to the hospital to see her by myself. By then she had completely lost all her functions. She was unable to open her eyes or speak. But somehow my mother knew I was there, because she shook her head in response to what I was saying to her. I told her that I loved her and that I forgave her.

I knew that deep down in my heart, she was sorry for everything she did in the past to me and my brothers, so all was forgiven and all grudges were put to rest. I also told her that I would make something of myself, no matter what, and that we as a family would always stick together.

Those were the last words I ever got to say to my mother. She died on March 11, 1995. Although my mother has passed on, I feel a part of her lives on in my sister. She knows what's going on. She's 5 and very smart for her age. I know there will come a time when my sister will pass on, too, but for now I take one day at a time. I accept all the negative things that have happened, focus on making a better life for me and my brothers, and I spend as much time with my sister as I can. Don't get me wrong, I miss my parents very dearly, but I try to only think about the good times, because it helps me to cope better.

I put my faith in God. I pray that He will stand guard over my family and protect us from the negative influences out in the streets. I strongly advise others who are going through what I have overcome to know the importance of letting your feelings out. Because once a person is gone, she's not coming back. If there is something you need to say, say it even if the person hates the truth.

A lot of times you might feel that what happened to you is all right. You may feel that you shouldn't say anything, because the person who committed the acts has suffered enough. Even if that's true, it is also important to let her know it wasn't all right and that she hurt you. Even though you forgive her, you should still get your anger off your chest. It is important to let that person know how you feel when they are alive, so that when they do pass on, you won't feel like you've been cheated.

My mother got a chance to hear we loved her. It wasn't because of guilt or because we knew she was going to die. It was just something we needed to say to her. My mother got to hear how we felt about the whole situation before she was put to rest.

I wrote a poem that I'm sure everyone can relate to:

A Frozen Mind

The shock of a sudden death
Makes some people feel
As if their minds are frozen.
This may be nature's way
Of protecting your mind,
So that everything can sink in
Slowly, and you won't be
Overwhelmed.
But if you talk to others and
Share your sadness,
Your mind will slowly begin to
defrost,
and you will start to adjust to your
loss.

Love Always,
Your Children

The Culture of Violence

Why I Love Gangsta Rap

By J. Slade Anderson

When you hear names like the Geto Boys, N.W.A, and Ice-T you probably think of woman-hating, violence-promoting monsters who get on a microphone and pour out streams of obscene language, threaten physical harm to anyone who opposes their ideas, and generally disrespect the people they don't like. In some ways this is true.

If you look up "hard-core" in the dictionary, the first definition you're likely to find is "extremely resistant to solution or improvement." Often, the word is used to describe criminals and people who are very, very angry. People who have nothing and have to scrounge around for food or fight to survive usually wind up becoming hard-core and a lot of hard-core rappers come from exactly that kind of background. Their families are poor, their neighborhoods are infested with drugs and violence. They suffer from both physical and mental poverty and after more than 400 years of oppression they feel trapped, powerless.

So they rap about rolling with gangs, pumps, TEC-9mm's, and Uzis. Some even go as far as to categorize White people as devils and threaten revenge.

The people who listen to them feel powerless too—often for a lot of the same reasons. If a cop ever hit you or treated you unfairly and you felt there was nothing you could do about it, you might be able to relate to Gangsta Nip when he raps about having to "get mean" and dismember the cop who slaps your mother. These angry poets give people a mental crutch for their damaged egos, a way to feel invincible, if only for a few minutes.

Even if you're not poor or Black and you don't live in the ghetto, you can still know something about powerlessness. Say you're the youngest in the family, for example, and people in authority are always yelling at you. Instead of ripping their vocal cords out, you might go into your room, shut the door, and put on a song like "F--k'em All" by the Geto Boys. And while you're in there, you feel strong enough to defend yourself. It's no substitute for a really strong self-image but it sure beats putting mind-altering poisons into your body or putting someone else down because you don't feel like a million bucks that particular day.

If someone rejects you or disrespects you, you could throw on some Gangsta Nip and listen to him "shoot you in the head and dip you in ammonia." It might feel good to imagine that person getting not only a taste of her own medicine but a barrel full of yours. That doesn't mean you're actually going to go out and kill anyone, but it sort of eases the pain just thinking about it.

I'm not saying I agree with everything these rappers say or that some immature listeners might not even take their words too much to heart and go out and do something stupid. I'll admit that some of these rappers don't know when they've made their point and go way overboard. On the other hand, if society would let all people have their normal strength and dignity without making some people feel like they have to prove it all the time, maybe then the beat would be the only hard thing about rap music.

Women Are Under a Rap Attack

By Yelena Dynnikov

Free expression receives a slap in the face whenever so-called "artists" use their First Amendment rights to demean women and send the message that we're all stupid tramps. The rap song "A B--ch Iz a B--ch" by N.W.A is a good example—it's just an endless stream of curses and physical threats. And Awesome Dre is anything but awesome in his rap "Sex Fiend." He seems to think that having sex with any girl he sees is his right: "Don't have to have permission 'cause I'm Awesome Dre." He believes women were created for the sole purpose of satisfying a man. I think he needs to change his name. How about Stone Age Dre, the caveman rapper?

When I hear songs like these, my jaw hardens and I shake with anger. I remember my first reaction to hearing Ice-T rap, "You know you want to do it too . . . you say you don't but I know you do." Fear rose up inside me. Are there really men out there who feel this way? I pressed the "stop" button on my Walkman to reassure myself that it could be stopped. That I could shut him up. But as silence filled the air, I questioned my action. What did I shut up—Ice-T or my Walkman? When guys on the street start following you and hassling you because they think you're good for only one thing, how do you shut them up? There's no stop button to use on them.

So many rap songs follow the same pattern—they create negative stereotypes of women and then use those stereotypes to legitimize treating women like dirt. It's an endless cycle. Women are first degraded and lowered: "Are you that funky, dirty, money-hungry, scandalous, stuck-up, hairpiece-wearing b--ch?" Raps like these suggest that women are plastic dummies with no brains, no ambitions, no personalities, and no feelings. They are portrayed by the "artists" as purely shallow sex toys. A girl's only function is to please the guy and after that she's discarded.

The rappers never want to get to know the women they pursue. In fact, they proudly admit that they're only after one thing. And if a woman doesn't leap at the chance, she is immediately branded a b--ch.

By now, you may be thinking, "What is she so worked up about? It's only music." It's because I think music is the only form of communication that really reaches a person. It steals the breath. It speaks to the heart. It moves the soul. It speaks even when no words are added and when accompanied by words, music can move boulders. It can also crash boulders if misused.

I hear lots of teens say that just because you hear something in a song does not mean that you'll go out and do it. Although that may be true, you can't deny that music can affect and influence a person subconsciously. Let's say a guy is out with a girl and wants to have sex with her. She says no, but another part of him is hearing Ice-T sing, "You say you don't want it but I know you do." A whole crew of rappers has hammered into his head the idea that you don't have to take what the girl says seriously, that having sex with who you want, when you want, is a guy's right. And anyway, deep down she really wants it, no matter what she says. The line between fantasy and reality may get confused. Some guys might start to think that saying no is just another way of saying "Convince me." But it's not. A guy who doesn't listen when a woman says no is a rapist.

Besides being ignorant and offensive, I think some of these songs put women in real danger. And even though I believe in freedom of expression, I have to admit there are times when I think censoring them just might be a good idea. Free expression is great as long as someone's got something to say. Preventing people from voicing their opinions on political and social issues like sexual preference, animal rights, or whether or not abortion should be legal is wrong and cannot be tolerated. But people who go around insulting and degrading women aren't standing up for what they believe in or making any important statement. I wish they could be censored, but I doubt that will happen.

There are other things that can be done, however. Look at what happened with Ice-T's song "Cop Killer." Whether or not you agree with the people who were offended by that song, you have to admit that they were effective—they got it taken off the album. If enough people complained about songs that are threatening to women, maybe we could get some of them taken off the air.

Refusing to buy and support those tapes is another way of fighting the stereotype of women they are putting out. If you hear an offensive song on the radio that hurts you personally, act on it. Call up the radio stations that play it and tell them that they have lost a listener because of that particular song. Write to the record company that produced it and tell them why you refuse to buy their records. A campaign like this can work if we make it work!

Diving into the Pit: I Came, I Saw, I Moshed

By Allen Francis

For years I have worn hip-hop hairstyles and clothes, used the appropriate slang, even written and performed my own raps. And since recently discovering alternative music, I have tried to honor my new love by experiencing everything it has to offer. I started wearing plaid shirts, playing air guitar, and swinging my head back and forth like the novice headbanger I was. But there was one thing I had yet to do: jump into the mosh pit.

Moshing is basically a bunch of people in a contained area pushing, hitting, and jumping into each other while listening to loud music. I got my first taste of moshing when I watched the MTV music awards a couple of years ago. Nirvana was performing "Lithium" and people were slamming into each other and a couple of guys climbed up on the stage and jumped into the crowd. At the time, I remember thinking, "Not a chance in hell . . ." But people change and now I wanted to do it. I felt that to fully appreciate the music, I had to experience how the people in the pit felt when the bodies started slamming.

I thought I'd have my chance over the summer when Biohazard (a hard metal band) was in town but my plans fell through. Then I attended an alternative concert in Central Park in the hopes that a pit would start, but it didn't. A little while later I found out that House of Pain, a rap group that's a favorite of mine, was appearing at Roseland, a club in Manhattan. Special guests: Biohazard and Korn. I was in there. When the night arrived, I was excited as hell. I was going to see House of Pain *and* mosh. My younger brother, Austin, and I arrived about an hour before the show was scheduled to start. Empty, Roseland looked huge. It was filling slowly but a quick head count confirmed that we were the only Black people there. This worried us a bit because there were some creepy-looking people in there. One guy had a Charles Manson shirt on.

By showtime there was still only a handful of Black people in the place, but we relaxed because we had come to have a good time, not cause trouble. I started talking to a guy who told me that the pit goes crazy for Biohazard, which almost made me reconsider. Korn was the opening act and I wasn't really interested in them because I didn't know who they were. But then I heard them and they were hype. They played heavy metal and the lead singer had these long dreadlocks that he swung back and forth violently to the music. He was enveloped in a red stagelight and I couldn't take my eyes off him. Until the pit started.

The pit is usually the area right in front of the stage. I was standing just to the side of it when I noticed that a couple of people had started crowd surfing—holding people aloft and passing them around on a sea of hands. Then I noticed that people had started slamming into each other and that got my full attention. The pit seemed dangerous. Some people with clenched fists were swinging their arms, not caring who they hit, and I didn't know what I was doing. Right around me everyone was calm, but about twenty feet away people were going crazy. With every moment the pit was swelling and getting bigger. If I didn't move, I would soon be swallowed by it.

I saw it coming toward me. All the calm people rushed away, but I said "F--k it." Then somebody pushed me from behind with his hands and I pushed the guy I ran into, and before I knew it, I was being pushed and hit from every direction. People fell on me, flailing arms hit me, and I kept getting shoved. My feet were getting caught in other people's legs. I pushed somebody, my head slammed into another head, and then some guy grabbed me. He hesitated for a second—maybe because I was the only Black guy in the pit—and then he pushed me a couple of feet. I remember getting a little angry, gritting my teeth, and pushing him off me. I had a minute to catch my breath and look at the stage before someone pushed me again.

I started pushing whoever I saw. Korn finished playing and I was still pushing people. It was like a high. I had never experienced anything like it before—violence that didn't get out of hand. It felt good to let off some steam, to express some of the anger inside of me. I was so excited I wanted to run out of the place, call someone, and yell, "I finally moshed!"

I found Austin where I left him, off to the side of the crowd. He saw me and said, "You're crazy, Al, I thought you was fighting that guy!" I told him I was on a buzz and asked him what he thought when he saw me mosh. "You're with your peoples," he said. "Crazy." I was ready to go back into the crowd but Austin decided to stay in his spot. He didn't want to get involved; watching was enough for him.

The crew was preparing the stage for Biohazard. I remembered that guy telling me that the pit goes wild for them. Meanwhile, I was concentrating on the people who were crowd surfing. It looked like fun, being carried aloft by everyone. I wanted to try it, but I didn't know how to start. I watched as five guys next to me got ready to lift someone. He pointed to a direction in the crowd and said, "That way." The guys threw him in the air and he crashed through a group of people before hitting the floor. "Why did they throw him?" I wondered. But was I discouraged?

I walked up to the guys and said, "Fellas, can you launch me?" "Newjack" must have been written all over me because one of them said, "Are you sure?" I said, "Yeah." He asked, "In which direction?" and I said, "I don't care." One guy cupped his hands to give me a leg up while the others grabbed me. I had one foot on the ground and used it to give myself a good jump.

I was up. It happened so fast I hardly remember it. I don't remember feeling hands but I know they were holding me up. I remember having this "I can't believe I'm doing this!" feeling. For about five or six seconds I was crowd surfing. Then, like Nine Inch Nails, I felt the "downward spiral" coming. My head and torso were going down. I couldn't get a handhold. I was yelling "AHHHHH," which turned into "SH-T!" as I landed on my back like the villain in a Bugs Bunny cartoon. One big guy gave me his palm and yanked me off the floor. That was it for me and crowd surfing.

Biohazard started playing and before I knew it I was in the maw of another pit. A forearm hit my upper back. I kept pushing and shoving but I was losing my breath and I felt a pain in my gut—the kind you feel when you run too fast for too long. I was getting exhausted and if I passed out I would get the living hell stomped out of me. I was trying to get out when I realized there was no way out. The whole ballroom was a pit. I panicked. What if Austin was in the middle of all this? I pushed and shoved my way out to the border, which was the wall. Austin and everyone that didn't want to mosh were pushed up against the wall. He seemed all right. I think he enjoyed being a neutral witness to the madness.

I joined him and looked back at the pit. It was a blur of people pushing and slamming into each other. Every couple of minutes I'd see two or three people surfing and Biohazard was blasting away. The scene was pure chaos and I loved it but I'd had my fill.

Biohazard finished and people were leaving in droves. There was finally some room to move. I left Austin again and got a good view of the stage for House of Pain. They were good but the music wasn't live; they used taped instrumentals as all rappers do. After seeing and hearing the live instruments of the other groups, it was a bit of a letdown. I felt Korn was the best.

I'll never forget that night. I'm a very outgoing person, but I don't usually get wild. I don't like hitting people, but it felt good to push and shove the people around me. It was like I was exploding for all the times I kept quiet to avoid an argument or backed down from a fight. For once, I let it all hang out. Still, I wouldn't recommend moshing for everybody. If you're not cautious you could get hurt or stomped out. I doubt if I will do it anytime soon. But I will do it again.

Gaybashers: What Are They Trying to Prove?

By Meliska Gruenler

In 1990, three young men lured Julio Rivera into a deserted schoolyard in Queens. Two of them beat him repeatedly with a hammer and a wrench, and the third stabbed him in the back. Then they left him there to die. The youths who murdered Rivera had two things in common: they were all between the ages of 15 and 25 and they all hated him because he was gay.

A lot of young guys feel threatened by gays and lesbians. They call them names, make jokes about them and some of them are responsible for attacks like the one against Rivera. Why would anyone hurt or kill someone just because that person is different? The most basic reason is fear, fear of the unknown. "People think we are a whole different species," said Angel Star, 20, a gay student at Harvey Milk High School in Manhattan. "Because you don't understand someone, you become afraid of him or her."

In the case of young men, who are often insecure about their sexuality, the fear is even greater. When some young men can't accept the possibility that they might be gay themselves, says Naomi Lichtenstein of New York City's Gay and Lesbian Anti-Violence Project, "They go out looking for targets, saying subconsciously, 'That one's the f--got, not me' . . . they literally want to get rid of the other person as a way of getting rid of the feelings in themselves. Of course it won't work; violence solves nothing."

Another reason is the pressure to be a "real man." A lot of young guys believe a man has to have sex with women and fight a lot. Most of these hate crimes start when a guy wants to prove to himself and his buddies that he's a man. So he'll say, "Let's go beat up a junkie or a f-g." Lichtenstein says older men tend to be more secure. "They don't need to prove anything," she explained. "And they've learned other ways of solving their own problems without hurting someone else."

But it's not just teens who are anti-gay, it's our whole society: parents, teachers, religion, the media—even the law. In movies and on TV young people see images of homosexuals as criminals and child molesters, according to Andy Humm of the Hetrick-Martin Institute for Gay and Lesbian Youth. It's practically forbidden to air programs that show two homosexual people touching.

The Roman Catholic Church teaches that it's wrong to be gay or lesbian and until recently the military threw people out if they were even suspected of it. In some states (not New York) there are still laws forbidding homosexuals to make love. Until 1973, the nation's psychiatrists considered being gay a mental illness.

There is such lack of understanding about homosexuals that even their parents often turn against them. Parents tell their kids, " 'I'd rather have a junkie than a gay son,' " says Angel, or " 'I'd rather you be a slut than for you to like girls.' . . . They'd rather have their child destroy their life and be miserable, than be gay."

It's no wonder a lot of teens grow up prejudiced against gays. Whether they learned those values at home, in church, in school, or from TV, homosexuality threatens a lot of people's "views on how the world should be," says Lichtenstein. Their belief in the traditional family is so narrow that anything else is wrong. So they go out and beat somebody up.

Experts agree the best way to change that is through education. Most people are not aware that surveys suggest that as many as one out of ten people in the United States is gay. "Society takes for granted [that] everyone is straight or that everyone should be," says Angel. People need to understand that it's normal to be gay, lesbian, or bisexual. "[It] doesn't make someone less of a man or woman," explains Lichtenstein. "A man or woman is not defined by who they love."

There was a time when Blacks were separated to the point where they had to use their own water fountains. Yet they drank the same water White people did. The only thing different about them was the color of their skin. Blacks went through a lot to prove they are equal. Well, gays are fighting a similar fight.

We all know that disliking someone because of color is being prejudiced and it's wrong. When teens think they're better than someone because he or she is gay, when they avoid the person or make rude comments, then they're being bigots just like the Ku Klux Klan. We are all human beings. Before you start to look for a reason to hate, look for a reason to love.

The Media War
Against Arabs

By Mohamad Bazzi

FBI and police officials say it is the center of a Middle East ter-
rorist conspiracy bent on destroying the American way of life.
They claim the shabby pulpit inside was used to preach a Muslim
jihad, or holy war, against Western civilization. Authorities are
quick to point out that Mohammed Salameh, one of the suspects
in the February 26, 1993, bombing of the World Trade Center,
might have worshiped there.

But the Al Salam mosque—spiritual home to Jersey City's Muslim community—is nothing more than a small room with little furniture that sits above an insurance company and gold trading store
along the bustling John F. Kennedy Boulevard. Inside, a makeshift
wooden pulpit stands in one corner, and the walls are lined with
shelves of holy books. There are no fancy benches or stained-glass
windows—just two glass chandeliers that hang from an old plaster
ceiling. Area Muslims (mostly Egyptians and Palestinians) say the
mosque is their only place of worship. They contend that their en-

tire culture is under attack and, considering past experience with anti-Arab racism in America, they're probably right.

On Friday, March 5, a day after Salameh's arrest and the Muslim holy day, people leaving afternoon prayer sessions at the mosque were surrounded by reporters and TV cameras. Out of anger and frustration, many refused to speak. The few who did spoke of being victimized and stereotyped. But the media didn't pay much attention. Neither did the guys who passed by the mosque that afternoon in trucks, shouting, "They should kill them all" and "Why don't you go back where you came from?"

The media siege continued for several days. So did dozens of prank calls and drive-by slurs. Then, on Sunday, March 7, Bronx Rabbi Avi Weiss led a protest across the street from the now infamous mosque. And a few days later, a Jersey City man was arrested and charged with breaking one of the mosque's windows.

How can all this happen without public outcry?

Arab-Americans have long been the forgotten minority of American society. That's why anti-Arab hate crimes surged during the Persian Gulf crisis—and may rise once again in the wake of the World Trade Center bombing. According to a report by the American-Arab Anti-Discrimination Committee (ADC), while only five hate crimes against Arab-Americans were reported for the first seven months of 1990, thirty-four such crimes were logged for the four months immediately following the Iraqi invasion of Kuwait in August. Nearly sixty hate crimes were reported in January 1991 alone, most of them after the war broke out. Many more cases, of course, went unreported.

Some in the ADC and other civil rights groups say things could have been worse. With nearly two and a half million Arab-Americans living throughout the country, the potential for widespread bigotry and hate crimes could have crippled the Arab community. Many believe that former president Ronald Reagan's "war on terrorism" of the 1980s (code words for a war on uncooperative Arabs and Muslims) laid the foundation for such a catastrophe.

But the problem of anti-Arab racism in America has even deeper roots. Arabs have been portrayed as the troublemakers of the Middle East since the end of World War II and the creation of Israel in 1948. The Gulf War was only the most recent example. From the outset of the huge military buildup against Iraq, Iraqi leader Saddam Hussein was portrayed as the Hitler of the Middle East—a madman bent on world domination and the destruction of Israel (thus reinforcing painful images and memories of the Holocaust). The demonization of Saddam Hussein went way beyond criticizing him and his policies. It was as if he were evil itself. Few TV and print news outlets explored the reasons for his popularity or gave the conflict any historical perspective.

That paved the way for gross anti-Arab racism in the press. *The New York Times,* for example, ran a disgusting cartoon on its opinion page during the height of the war titled, "The Descent of Man." It showed Hussein as lower than a snake on the chain of evolution. He was dirty and had a cloud of flies around his head. Organizations like Fairness and Accuracy in Reporting (FAIR) blasted the cartoon as racist. FAIR said the cartoon is reminiscent of Nazi propaganda that presented Jews as subhuman, and KKK propaganda that portrays Blacks as related to apes. The cartoon also implied that Hussein (a national leader) was genetically inferior—a slur against all Arabs. It was a fitting statement for the most respected newspaper in a country where many see Arabs as "ragheads" who ride around the desert on camels lusting after White women.

This kind of stereotyping seems to have reemerged in the past few weeks. For instance, the *Daily News* last month ran a front-page photo of a bearded Salameh, the Trade Center bombing suspect, under a headline that screamed: "Face of Hate." *New York Newsday* ran the same picture with the headline "Portrait of a Loser."

But some journalists still had enough sense to see through the anti-Arab paranoia. "Even *The New York Times* could not resist describing bombing suspect Mohammed Salameh's 'beakish nose.' Would the paper dare mention a Jewish suspect's 'beakish nose'? Or a Black suspect's 'thick lips'? Or a 'slant-eyed' Asian suspect?" Betty Liu Ebron wrote in the *Daily News.*

Of course not!

Violent Times, Violent Movies

By Daniel Jean-Baptiste

Over the last year or so, a lot of films have come out that deal with the impact of gangs, drugs, and violence on city youth. The news media have criticized some of these movies—particularly *New Jack City* and *Juice*—for encouraging real-life violence. An editorial in *The New York Times* stated that "films like *Juice* are clearly packaged to appeal to the most violent segments of the audience."

I disagree. Movies such as *Juice* attempt to realistically portray the problems faced by city youth. They don't promote violence. These movies show the downside of using or dealing drugs and joining gangs, and show that there are alternatives. *Juice* is about four teenage guys who do everything together. They consider themselves a crew, not a gang. In the beginning all they do is cut school, hang out, and shoplift. They aren't violent. They don't jump other kids and they don't carry guns. But anger, peer pressure, and one crew member's obsession with "juice" push them further.

First, they decide to rob a store—because they want money and because they want to teach the store owner a lesson for always chasing them away from his place with a gun. One of the guys, GQ, doesn't want to go through with it but he's pressured by his friends. To pull off the robbery, the guys decide they need a gun because they know the store owner has one. They don't plan on shooting the man, but Bishop (the kid obsessed with juice) ends up killing him anyway. After they all get away from the scene of the crime, Rahim, the leader of the crew, tries to take the gun away from Bishop. Instead of giving it up, Bishop kills him.

Watching the movie, you don't admire Bishop. He is like the villain—the kid on the wrong track. The guy that the audience cheers for is GQ, the one who didn't want to get involved in the robbery in the first place. What sets GQ apart from the other crew members, especially Bishop, is that he has a goal in life—he wants to be a DJ. It's not what his mother really wants for him, but it's an honest goal. GQ doesn't want the type of respect that one gets by having a bad reputation on the streets. He wants the type of respect that one gets for working hard at being the best in something.

Bishop is another story. The movie shows how, because of his insatiable desire for power, nothing else is important to him—not even the lives of his friends. An advertising poster for *Juice* read: "Juice. Power. Respect. How far will you go to get it?" Through Bishop, the movie shows the consequences of going too far.

New Jack City is another movie that deals directly with drugs, gangs, and violence. It's about a family of drug dealers who invent the "perfect drug" and use it to monopolize the local drug trade. They murder their way to the top and continue murdering to stay on top. Eventually they begin to betray and kill each other. In the beginning of the film, the head of the family, Nino Brown, frequently asks, "Am I my brother's keeper?" and all the members of his drug organization answer in unison: "Yes, I am." We find out that these are just words later in the movie, when Brown's brother unknowingly hires an undercover cop who ends up destroying the organization.

The brother comes to apologize to Nino, who begins to cry

but doesn't hesitate to take out his gun. The brother asks, "Am I my brother's keeper?" Brown thinks for a while, says, "Yes, I am," and shoots his brother. At the end of the film Nino Brown gets a taste of his own medicine when he is killed by a citizen determined to bring him to justice. *New Jack City* clearly illustrates that drug dealing and drug abuse both lead to undesirable and destructive ends. Nino Brown has the money, the cars, and the girls, but he loses it all. The movie shows that any gain achieved through dealing is merely temporary.

While addressing the drug dealing, the movie also shows you the intensity of drug addiction. A drug dealer who is less successful than Nino Brown becomes addicted to his product and, as a result, loses everything. He goes into rehab to try to kick his habit, but after months of struggling to set himself straight, the mere sight of drugs rekindles his addiction. The message of this segment of the movie is: Don't try drugs at all because prevention is far better than the cure.

It's true that both these movies depict violent acts. Unfortunately, violence is a problem in our society; we can't pretend it doesn't exist. And these films don't just show the violence, they show the consequences of violent behavior. This makes for an effective anti-violence, anti-drug message. If the theaters were showing a "Read my lips, don't do drugs" message by George Bush, then the youth of America would not pay $7.50—or any price at all—to go see it. The message wouldn't be taken seriously if it were coming from a person who didn't really know how it is. It is because these movies are dramatic, entertaining, and realistic that the audience will sit there for over an hour and watch them. Watching these films, you might even say to yourself, "These people who made this really know what the deal is."

The basic message conveyed by *Juice* and *New Jack City* is similar to the one contained in lectures we get from our parents, the public service commercials we see on television, and the lessons we get in health class. Same message, different packaging. And the difference in the packaging will make young people more likely to listen and learn.

Hoods n' the Boys

By Karina Sang-Petrillo

Have you noticed that there are more and more kids around who wear hoodies, baggy clothes, expensive sneakers and jackets, and caps with team names on them? I have to admit I had a stereotype about these guys. I thought that everyone who dressed that way spent their time hanging out on street corners, wasting their lives away. I called them "hoods."

A number of teens I interviewed had negative things to say about these guys. Tina Law, 17, of Columbus High School, said they look like "bums on the street." Carlo Torres, 17, of Francis Lewis High School, said, "They look like drug dealers." But Carlo also told me that not everyone who dresses like a hood is a criminal. "Not all of them are tough," he said. "Everybody just wants to look like that. They think it gets them respect or something."

I decided to ask some guys who looked like hoods to me how they felt about these stereotypes. At first I was a little afraid to approach them because I pictured them as violent people who would refuse to talk to me. But I found out that I had worried for nothing. All the "hoods" I talked to were pretty nice (except for one guy I found very insulting because he started making comments about sex while I was interviewing him). I approached guys who were dressed in what I thought was the typical hood fashion: the baggy pants, the hoodie, the expensive sneakers, hats, short close-shaved hair, and leather and Starter coats. None of them reacted violently, but some guys who do not consider themselves hoods did get very insulted by my questions.

A lot of the guys I spoke to contradicted themselves, first by saying that they were not hoods, then by saying they were because they had to be. Like Jasun, 15, of Evander Childs High School. First he told me that he didn't think he was a hood and that it was all a style of dressing. Then he told me that what made him a hood was "the life I'm living. Robbing, always getting blisted, smoking blunts, drinking forties." Well, which is it?

Most of the self-declared hoods I talked to blamed their lifestyle on the neighborhood they grew up in. Some blamed it on pressure from friends and the desire to fit in and be respected. Pete, 17, of Evander Childs High School, described hoods as people who "go out and rob stores." Pete admitted he had been to jail himself for assault and robbery but said, "I don't really consider myself a hood. If somebody wants problems I will give it to them." Lenster, 16, also from Evander Childs, gave me a similar definition. He said he was a hood "cause I'm a criminal. [I] steal cars, stick up people."

But many other people said that you don't have to commit a crime to be a hood, that it's only a way of dressing. "It's the style. It's stylish and the girls like it," said Lonniu Daughtry, 14, of Alfred E. Smith High School. Michael Martin, 19, said that being a hood was just "an attitude."

Given the negative impression that a lot of people have of hoods, why would someone choose to dress that way if he weren't a criminal? "He wanna be down, dress like them, act like them," Lonniu said. "Probably to get attention from them."

The non-hood students I interviewed felt that being a hood was more than a fashion statement. "They hang out on any street corner. They commit petty crimes and try to get laid," said Cynthia Ortiz, 17, of Columbus High School. The guys who consider themselves hoods agreed with most of this statement. They said they do hang out on street corners and most of the ones I interviewed had been to jail.

But Michael Martin also said, "You can call me anything you want. Cause I know I'm not a hoodlum. I probably dress like one." Jasun had something similar to say. "People just call people things. Those are just words," he said.

I would still call someone who hangs out on street corners, committing petty crimes and wasting his life away, a hood. But doing interviews for this story taught me that I shouldn't automatically assume someone does those things because of the way he dresses. A lot of guys who fit the hood image are not criminals. In fact, some of the guys I was scared to approach for interviews turned out to be very friendly and fun. The problem is that while being a "hood" can be just a style, it can also be a way of life. And some of guys I talked to didn't seem sure themselves whether they were acting the part or just wearing the costume.

A Gassed-Up Head Is Dangerous

Choices

Letters to Parents

Dear Mom,

Remember the last three years when I used to work in the print shop? I used to tell you I had to work extra hours for money. Well, it was true, but I was earning dirty money by selling drugs.

Every weekend I used to come with gold and nice clothes. You'd ask me for the receipt and I said I ripped it. Remember when you asked me how much I used to earn for extra hours?

Remember that time I didn't come home for three days? My friend Slinky and I had to go and get some money in Crotona Park after work. When I went to a project to get money the Dominican guys started shooting, and they shot me in my behind and cut just a little. I twisted my ankle while running.

Mom, I never told you about selling drugs cause it was sad. You know that I love you a lot. I also didn't tell you about my girls because that was sad too.

Well, now I would like to tell you who I really like from my school. She is Betsy C.

Your son

Dear Mom,

I have a drug problem and it's really serious. That's why I never have any money. And the baby never has Pampers. It's because of the coke I sniff.

After I'm high I like to have sex and I know that's not good because of all the diseases that are going around. Mom, please help me because I have a daughter that I have to raise and I want to be a good mother to my child.

Betsy (name changed)

We Wanted Revenge

By Carlos López

It was the last day before Christmas vacation. I was walking home when I saw an ambulance and cop cars by the 7-Eleven. I walked past, figuring it probably wasn't any of my business. Then I saw Joe, a friend of mine from way back. He walked up to me and blurted out, "David got stabbed."

At first I didn't believe it. David? My friend David? Stabbed? This made no sense. Things like that didn't happen to the people I knew. They just flashed across a television screen. They didn't happen in real life.

But it had happened. The ambulance was there to pick up David, and the cop cars were there to find out what had happened.

It seemed that some guy had taken David's chain, a fake gold chain he wore everywhere. When the guy took off, David ran after him. As he got close, the guy turned and stabbed him. David lay there bleeding and the guy got away. They never caught him.

At first I couldn't believe it had happened at all. But as I was going home, I began to get angry, infuriated. I felt helpless. Here this guy had gotten away and David was left bleeding in the middle of the street. I wanted to find the guy and kill him.

I wasn't the only one. That night I went out with John, a friend of both David and me, and we hung out in a park by his house drinking. We were both upset that the guy who stabbed David had gotten away. We couldn't do anything; David almost got killed and the guy gets away. We wanted revenge.

The next day, a few more people got together with John and me. I didn't know most of them, but most of them knew David. Everyone was out to kill someone. We were going to get in a car, cruise around the neighborhood where he got stabbed, and find the guy who did it. But the only thing that we had to go on was that he was Hispanic, had short brown hair, and was pretty muscular.

At first I was willing to go along. Then I started to think about what we were doing—we were looking for someone to fit a general description, and it occurred to me that we would probably hurt an innocent person. "This is insane," I told them. But they didn't listen. Most of them were just out for a fight. They didn't care who they fought. But John and I couldn't deal with hurting an innocent person. We were still angry, but we weren't going to go out and hurt someone who might just be in the wrong place at the wrong time. So we left. (Of course, there were a few snide remarks from some of the people in the mob.)

From what I understand, all they ended up doing was driving around until they got tired and eventually wound up in a club somewhere. David was in the hospital for a month. When he got out he was fine, and everyone pretty much forgot about the incident. But sometimes I think about what might have happened if I had gone with them and if we had found someone who fit the description.

A Proud Moment:
Turning In a Killer

By Anonymous

The names in this story have been changed.

About two years ago, I attended a summer camp in Crown Heights. As the summer went by I became close to a guy named George. He had many enemies. Guys were jealous of him because he had money, gear, and girls. One particular kid, Sean, didn't like George. He and his friends constantly accused George of messing around with their girlfriends. One day, after camp, Sean and his friends attacked George, robbed him, and shot him. They left him for dead just two blocks from the camp. Everyone knew it was Sean, but nobody wanted to put their life on the line.

I didn't want to say anything either, but as the days passed it picked and ate at my brain and my conscience grew louder with every thought of George. I cried myself to sleep every night. Then I saw Sean sporting one of George's chains and I snapped. Still, no one else came forward to tell. After being questioned for the umpteenth time, I broke down in tears as I told the detective and cop what I knew, heard, and saw.

My parents and George's were the only ones who knew it was me. It took almost two weeks and a lot of guts to do it because I feared for my life. But to this day I'm proud and glad I did. I'm positively sure George would have done the same for me.

George, I love and miss you.

R.I.P.

Why I Carry a Gun

By Anonymous

I got my first gun when I was 13 because I thought it was cool. I didn't really have any use for one at the time but I knew a lot of people who had guns and I wanted one too. The gun was a .25 automatic. I got it from my friend for $100.

It's easy to get a gun in my neighborhood. There are guys all over who sell them. I never used mine to hurt anybody. The most I did was go up on the roof of an abandoned building and shoot a few cans and bottles.

I'm 17 now and my reasons for carrying a gun have changed. I live in a really rough area of Brooklyn and I've seen a lot of things. Once I went to a party in Flatbush. Everybody was dancing and having a good time and then shots rang out and everyone ran outside. (Luckily no one got hurt.) Another time I heard shots outside my window. I looked out and saw this man chasing another man down the street, shooting. I've been stuck up a couple of times myself and friends of mine have been shot dead.

Once I shot a guy in self-defense. I was at a party minding my business when a boy walked up to me and said he had heard that I was messing with his girl.

"What the hell you talking about?" I said. "I don't know you nor your damn girl."

He turned to some other guys and said, "Yo, I got him." I knew something was gonna go down, so I left.

After I got outside, I noticed some guys following me. I ran and hid in a bushy area until they had gone by. All the time my hand was on my gun—just in case.

After they were gone, I stepped out from where I was hiding, and just then another guy came around the corner heading in the same direction as his friends. He saw me and reached into his coat. I fired twice. He fell on the ground with his gun in his hand. If I hadn't shot him first I might not be here today.

I've had lots of guns. I just plain lost the first one. After that there were a couple of times when I had to get rid of a gun because I was scared the cops were going to find it on me. Cops in my neighborhood are always stopping a group of kids and searching them. One time I was hanging out with my friends and I saw the cops drive by. I had a feeling they were coming back so I dropped my gun down the sewer. They did come back and found guns on all my friends and drove them off to jail.

Later that same night I went out to get something to eat and this group of kids robbed me. One of them stuck a gun in my stomach and they pushed me up against the wall and went digging through my pockets. They took all my money and ran off. I was so mad that I went home and got another gun I had and went back out after them. I didn't find them. I was glad I didn't because that would've brought trouble on me from the cops.

There are a lot of ways just having a gun can bring trouble. For one thing, you have to be careful where you get it. You don't want a gun with "bodies on it." With a gun in your pocket you can also be tempted to do stupid things. Some people use their guns to show off and make themselves look big—that's foolishness. You might shoot someone you don't like or try to take revenge. And if other people know you have a gun they're more likely to try to shoot you before you get the chance to shoot them.

Editors' Note: Two months after writing this article, the author was arrested for allegedly pointing a handgun at a fellow student in the bathroom of their high school.

Why I Don't Have a Gun

By Anonymous

Nowadays teenagers get firearms without any problem and then end up using them stupidly. They kill each other as if life were some kind of Nintendo game where you can press Reset and then start all over again.

Life is not like that. People should ask themselves why they choose to own a gun in the first place and think very carefully before shooting one. We need to stop the violence. It's messed up and it's getting us nowhere. It got a friend of mine killed.

It was a Saturday night about a year ago. I went to a jam. At around 1 a.m., the two girls whose party it was threw everyone out. I was already outside, taking my stereo home, when I heard a shot. I looked back to see what had happened, and I saw my friend Tony. He told me that he had some kind of disagreement with the two girls and shot a 9mm into the house just to scare them.

"What if you would have shot one of the girls?" I asked him.

"I don't care," he said.

When he said that, I thought this guy was crazy. We walked to my house and Tony left. By this time it was 2:30 in the morning and I headed toward a store back near where the party had been.

When I got there I saw the two girls Tony had the argument with. One of them was pregnant and was crying. "What if that bullet would have killed me or my unborn baby?" she said. I rubbed her belly and told her that I was sorry. I didn't know he was going to shoot in the house. Then I went to my friend's house thinking it was all over. It wasn't.

I was with another friend, Luis, trying to get the door of his house open, when I heard an ambulance racing down the street. My friend went to see what happened, and came back and told me: "Tony, Paco. It's Tony!" I ran over and Tony was dead.

The way the story goes, the pregnant girl called her brother and the two of them, along with another friend, waited for Tony on his block. When he got there, the two guys confronted Tony. "Why did you shoot at my sister?" the brother asked. Tony denied doing it. The pregnant girl wanted her brother to scare him by putting a gun to his head while she smacked him.

Unfortunately it didn't go like they planned. Tony wasn't scared; he thought the guy was only joking. He recognized him and said, "Oh I know you, you live in . . ." and pushed the gun away.

"I'm not playing," the guy said and pointed the gun at Tony again. I'm not sure what happened next, but according to witnesses, Tony pushed the gun away again. Then they opened fire. They shot Tony a couple of times in the legs and knees. While Tony was on the ground against the wall, they shot him in the neck and head.

After seeing what happened to Tony and many other friends of mine, my choice has been not to own a gun. A gun is a very risky item to have. First you waste $200, $300, or even $400 for something you will barely use. And let's say you do happen to use it and you shoot or even kill someone. What do you think is going to happen next? You'd go crazy worrying whether or not you have people looking for you to kill you for revenge and you'd probably have to spend most of your life in JAIL.

There's another reason I don't want a gun: When you own a gun you feel more powerful than everyone else. It gets your head all gassed up and a gassed-up head is dangerous. It could explode on you. Just like you, other people also make the choice of owning a gun and when you least expect it, they end up shooting you. That is a chance you should not take.

Editors' Note: This article was adapted from two separate articles submitted to us in the mail. Because we were unable to contact the writer and confer with him, we have published it without his name and have changed all names and a few of the details as well.

I Carry Mace . . .
Just in Case

By Anonymous

Coming home after dark to my messed-up neighborhood never really scared me. Even on winter nights when the sky instantly turns pitch dark at 5 p.m., I would walk by myself through crack alleys and past junkie houses just because the route was shorter. I never thought about getting beat up, shot, or killed.

I wasn't worried about these things but my mother sure was. After watching an episode of *Oprah* about stalkers and a *Code 3* segment about a teenage girl who was alone in the house when a robber broke in, she kept telling me that these things could happen to me.

After that, my mother and I began discussing our fears. We both agreed that the thing we were most scared of was getting raped. We knew if that happened we would feel violated, mad at ourselves, and afraid to step outside. It was an intense conversation and not once did my mother call me a moron for feeling the way I did. Not even when I suggested that maybe we should both get some type of protection.

The following week my mother surprised me by handing me a can of Mace. "Here," she said, "and don't abuse it." I was shocked. My mother was serious about this. Then she showed me the stun gun she had bought for herself. I was amazed. But I figured if my mother cared so much about the issue of protecting herself, then I should too.

Talking to my mother about rape is the thing that really got to me. I think rape is even scarier than death because after you're dead, you can't feel guilty or ashamed or anything. With rape, you live with the pain, anger, and hurt for the rest of your life. My mother understands my fears because she feels them herself. That's why she got me the Mace.

I know some people will think it's weird that my mother got me a weapon, but since she and I live alone, who's going to protect me from the evil clutches of the world? My mommy can't because she works most of the day. She thought I needed to become my own bodyguard.

I'm glad to say that, so far, I've never used the Mace on anyone. But just having it makes me feel more secure. When I see a guy that's weird looking, I put my hand in my pocket and hold tightly onto my Mace. It gives me more strength and confidence and makes me feel like I have something that'll back me up if I'm ever in trouble. It's like a friend who has your back in a fight. That's what it is, my best friend during the night.

I'm determined to use the Mace *only* if a guy tries to physically harm me. I don't think I'd use it on another girl because I know I would have a fighting chance without it. But if a guy pushes me or pulls my arm or follows me that's when I'd use it.

The great part about Mace is that, unlike a gun, it can't kill anyone. That's why it's my kind of weapon. Even so, I worry that something might go wrong. The thought of the Mace backfiring disturbs me. What if I use it and I don't spray enough of it or I turn the knob to the wrong side and spray myself? What will I do? I'm not exactly she-hulk. I'm petite and I look breakable, so fighting back is not my idea of saving my own life. I figure running is going to have to be my backup—so legs, don't fail me now.

I don't flaunt that I have it because I don't want anyone to think that I'm Ms. Bad Girl and I'm so tough. Actually, I know many girls that have Mace, stun guns, guns . . . so I'm not so extraordinary. A lot of girls carry some kind of weapon for the same reasons I do. They don't want to get hurt by some strange lunatic. I see my Mace as something that can help me out of a situation that I don't want to be in. So unless you have money to pay for my kung fu lessons, I'll stick with it.

Editors' Note: Carrying chemical Mace is illegal in many states, and even pepper sprays cannot be given to minors.

My Secret Habit

By Anonymous

When I was 15, I gained twenty pounds in a matter of months. After breaking up with my boyfriend, I started eating like a pig. By May I looked like a total slob—and swimwear season was coming! I was miserable.

Meanwhile, my ex was parading around with his new girlfriend. Of course she was thin, which made me even more upset. But there was nothing I could do about it except continue stuffing my face.

One day, as I was drowning my sorrows in yet another pint of ice cream, I overheard my friend Cheryl (not her real name) talking to her cousin. Cheryl was thin, too. "It's so easy," she was saying. "Whenever you feel full, or when you feel guilty about eating pizza or"—she glanced at me—"ice cream, just go to the bathroom, and throw up. You'll feel light again."

Her cousin and I stared at her in disgust. "That's stupid,

Cheryl," I said. You just can't throw up whenever you want, I thought.

Or can you?

The answer to my question came as soon as I finished dinner that night. Cheryl's words "You'll feel light again" stuck in my head as I went into the bathroom. I stared at the toilet for at least ten minutes before I did anything. I leaned over the toilet bowl slowly, hearing the laughter coming from the living room, where my family was watching *Beetlejuice.*

I stuck one finger down my throat. Nothing happened. I stuck a second, then a third, and then it all came rushing out of me. It was not the easiest thing in the world, but Cheryl was right. I felt light and empty, and I wasn't even hungry! My summer might not be that bad after all.

That's how I began my "little phase," as I like to call it. Every day, after dinner, I'd slip into the bathroom. I'd run the water in the tub, so no one could hear what I was doing. Then I'd hurl away. The guilt I had about overeating left me along with the food.

After two weeks of this I looked at the scale. All I had lost was a ridiculous four pounds. Four pounds! I cried myself to sleep that night, fearing the worst—that I would be fat forever. Was that possible? With so many thin and beautiful women in the world, why couldn't I be like them?

I started throwing up after every single meal, big or small, although most of them were huge. My "little habit" made it easier for me to eat all the food I wanted, because it would soon be gone anyway. I would eat five or six slices of pizza, sometimes more, plus ice cream by the ton, cookies, cakes, everything I could get my hands on. After each feast, I'd head for the bathroom.

After another two weeks, I looked at the scale again, and I'd lost ten pounds! I was so happy, especially since everybody started paying me compliments about the way I looked. Cheryl was right. It was so easy.

Then, in late June, I noticed the bruises. Large black and blue marks were covering my arms and legs, and I had no idea how or why I was getting them. I also realized that I was in pain. My right side was killing me all the time and I had to lie down a lot. My period stopped for a while. And I started to have frequent bad dreams. I would wake up in a cold sweat, wondering what was happening to me. A slight fear would run through me, because I didn't know what was wrong, but at that point I didn't really care. I refused to accept that I had a problem. All I wanted was to be as thin as I possibly could.

My "little habit" was affecting my personality as well as my body. I became extremely moody and irritable, and I would constantly yell at my brother and my mom. All I wanted was for them to leave me alone with my food. I would send my mom to the store to buy me something, then I'd eat and eat, and throw up before she got home. I had no social life, no hobbies. My life revolved around this obsession I had with food.

Still, no one seemed to notice that anything was wrong with me. If they did, they didn't say anything. My friends noticed that I was going to the bathroom all the time, but I'd just make some excuse about being on a water diet.

In July, I heard the news: Cheryl was in the hospital. At first I thought she had an accident or something, but when I called her house, her brother told me the truth. Her mother caught her throwing up and dragged her to the hospital, kicking and screaming. They found out that she had anorexia nervosa (a disorder in which a person becomes so obsessed with dieting and thinness that she starves herself) and bulimia (when a person follows a pattern of eating a huge amount of food and then throwing up or taking laxatives to get rid of it). Cheryl's weight had dropped down to eighty-five pounds on a five-foot-seven frame, but her mom never realized her problem until she caught Cheryl in the act.

My mom went off when she found out. "I don't want you hanging around with that girl anymore! How could her mother not know what was wrong with her?" She continued ranting for about an hour, but I ignored her. My mom didn't realize I had the same problem as Cheryl, and now I knew not to tell her. She would kill me, and I would never hear the end of it.

I sat down and thought about what I was doing to myself, and what was happening to Cheryl. There was no comparison, I told myself. Her problem was way bigger than mine. But then I tried to remember: when was the last time I ate a decent meal without throwing up afterward? Almost four months ago. That's when I realized I had a serious problem. That day I decided to quit, because I didn't want to end up like Cheryl.

Stopping was much harder than starting had been. I still remember the first time I sat down to eat dinner after making my decision. Once it was over, I automatically got up to go to the bathroom, but I made myself sit down again. That was probably one of the hardest things I ever had to do.

I decided to go to the doctor, praying that my mother wouldn't have to know. Luckily, my doctor is a very understanding person. She counseled me and gave me a list of healthy things to eat. She gave me her phone number at home so I could call if I had any problems.

By the time I quit making myself throw up, I had lost almost fifty pounds (my goal when I started out was to lose thirty). I know I've gained some of it back but I don't look at the scale anymore. My doctor tells me not to. No one really knows about my problem, except my doctor, and I'd like to keep it that way. I know my family and friends couldn't handle it.

It's been almost a year since I stopped, and I feel much better about myself now. My health is much better. I don't have as many mood swings. All the marks and the bad dreams are gone. And my social life is a lot better. Sometimes I still feel that I would like to lose more weight, but my thoughts go back to seeing Cheryl lying on that hospital bed.

After all I went through to have the "ideal body," I can now easily say that it wasn't worth the isolation and the pain. Being thin doesn't mean being happy.

I Hated Myself

By David Miranda

By the time I was eleven, I already knew I was gay and I hated myself for it. I hated myself so much that I wanted to kill myself. I wanted to be "normal." I didn't want God to punish me and give me AIDS. I didn't want to go to hell.

Every day after school I would go to church. "Please give me the strength to change myself," I would pray. "Please, please, please." I always expected God to answer me but She or He never did. I remember one day at school one of the kids in my class asked a teacher, "Does God always answer your prayers?" The teacher replied, "Yes, no matter what, in one form or another God will always answer your prayers." Not mine.

I even made a vow that if God would make me heterosexual I would become a priest. After church I would go home and read the entire Bible. All I remember about being 11 is praying. Every Saturday I went to confession. I would confess everything except that I had gay feelings. On Sundays I made sure I went to mass. None of it worked.

"Why me?" I'd ask myself over and over again. I saw myself as a freak of nature, and as a devil. All that I ever knew about gay men at the time were the stereotypes and lies that my parents taught me: that they were child molesters and wanted to be women.

"*Siéntate bien,*" my father would tell me. "*Camina como hombre.*" (Learn how to sit right. Walk like a real man.) He said these things to me so many times that I can still hear him.

My parents taught me that gay people were not people at all. Driving through the West Village I remember them laughing at the "*maricas,*" and trying to imitate gay people, by saying "*Ay, chus,*" and acting like stereotypical homosexuals. This taught me that gay people didn't deserve any respect. So how was I supposed to feel when I discovered that I was gay? How is one supposed to feel when you find out that you are a freak, a pervert, a piece of human sh-t?

One day I told my friend John (not his real name) that I was planning to kill myself. I asked him how I should do it. "Why don't you try mothballs?" he said. John was supposed to be my best friend. I figured that if my best friend didn't care whether or not I died then no one would. I knew that I was alone and that there was no one I could turn to. I was scared of people.

That's when I made up my mind to do it. I was scared and felt I didn't deserve to live. It was as if there were a knife lodged in my chest that I couldn't take out. I thought about different ways to kill myself. I went to my roof and looked down but I was too scared to jump. I figured that Windex could kill a person, so I drank a whole bottle. It didn't even make me sick.

Then I decided to swallow a whole bottle of Tylenol. I drank it down with iced tea, and every time I took another pill I felt glad that I was that much closer to death and that much further from having to live a miserable life. I closed my eyes and went to sleep hoping it was all over and I'd never have to wake up again.

All I remember from that night was waking up in the darkness every half hour to throw up. I felt as if there was some monster inside of me that just wanted to come out. I remember leaning over the toilet bowl and feeling dirty, and hearing my father say, "Let it out, let it out, you'll feel better." But I just kept throwing up over and over again.

The next morning when I opened my eyes, I felt as if I had spent a night in hell. I realized that nothing had changed. I still had to deal with my stepmother, and on Monday I'd have to deal with the a--holes at school again who always brought up the word "f--got."

I went to a guidance counselor and, without telling her that I was gay, told her what happened. I made up a story about a friend dying. By that time I already knew that the best way to keep my secret was by lying.

The counselor called my father and he rushed to school. She told me to step outside while she talked to him. I waited anxiously wondering what my dad would do when he came out.

Instead of yelling at me, my normally grumpy father was nicer than I'd ever seen him before. "You're my son and I love you," he told me. "Why would you do something so stupid?" You could tell that he was trying to do everything in his power not to upset me. In a way I was glad because he was giving me a lot of attention. He took me out to eat, and talked about moving out of New York City. But in another way it was so fake that it made me uncomfortable.

The guidance counselor told him that I needed to go to the hospital, because there was a possibility that the Tylenol could have done physical damage. At least that was the excuse that they gave me to convince me to go to a psychiatric hospital for three months.

I will never forget the fears that went through my mind when they told me I would have to go to a mental hospital. I imagined a place full of crazy people who would try to hurt me. I also imagined a deranged psychiatrist who would put doses of harmful medication in my food. But it turned out that the three months I spent at the hospital were actually fun. I woke up every morning and went to group meetings and activities. It was the first time that I actually had friends. Up to that time I had tried my hardest to avoid other people my age. I felt that nobody would like me. I hated people.

At the hospital I was with people who actually liked me. They were all older, about 16 or 17, and to them I was the cute little kid. I enjoyed the way they were treating me. During meals we would talk and I would laugh. I know that doesn't sound like much but laughing and being happy was a rare feeling for me in those days. At the end of each day we would go to the gym and work out. It was all a lot of fun. And my parents were nicer to me than they had ever been before.

After three months I was out of the hospital. I had lied my way through the whole therapy, saying that my only problems were my best friend who had committed suicide, the fact that I had no friends, and that I hated myself. The one time the subject of homosexuality came up I just said, "It's weird. I don't understand how anyone can not like women." They believed everything and then sent me to live with my mother in Brooklyn.

In Brooklyn I found new friends. I continued to live a lie, however. One day I went home and swallowed another bottle of Tylenol, for no reason other than to make myself suffer through another hellish night. Another time I took twenty of my mother's blood pressure pills. I felt that I had no reason to live. My vision of myself as an adult was as a lonely, miserable person who would never be accepted by society. The idea of dying in my sleep was very attractive.

I would go to school and chill with my friends and we'd lie to each other about how many girls we'd had. I got into a lot of fights because at that age kids would call each other f--got. I would get extremely offended by this word, and I would beat up anyone who said it to me. Some of my friends would ask me, "Why do you get so offended when people call you f--got if you know you're not?"

I started asking girls out, and lying to myself by telling myself that girls were my thing. I started to date them and I enjoyed it. I enjoyed them as far as friendship was concerned but I didn't see it going beyond that.

Junior high school was a total flop for me. I did everything to prove my manhood. I stole cars, picked fights, and went on rampages in the train, "catching herbs" with older kids and cutting school. I went from class nerd to most likely to drop out.

I got out of it all when I decided to go to a high school that was outside my neighborhood. All of my "friends" were going to the neighborhood high school, so I now had the chance to go and make some new friends in a place where nobody knew anything about me.

On my first day a question was haunting me: "What if people find out?" I was terrified out of my mind. At first I made many friends but then I would close up and stop talking to them. I was so afraid of being found out that I would stop going to school just so that I didn't have to deal with people. When I did go I started monitoring my every move. I would be scared to talk, walk, or even look at anyone. I felt as if I had the word "f--got" stamped on my forehead. Eventually I was put in "holding power," which is a nice way of saying truant class. I was just waiting for my 16th birthday so that I could drop out.

It was during high school that I found that I needed a place to meet other gay people. I knew there were places like that out there, but I didn't know how to get in touch with them. I decided that I was going to ask a guidance counselor for places to go. I wasn't sure whether it was the right thing for me to do. I kept thinking about it for weeks. What if he called my parents? What if he laughed at me? What if they threw me out of school?

Finally I arranged to talk with a guidance counselor. My heart raced and my palms were sweaty as I prepared to tell the first person ever about my big secret.

"How can I help you?" Mr. Smith, my guidance counselor, asked me.

"I have a very big problem," I said. Then came the big bomb: "I think I might be gay."

He just smiled and said, "And?"

My first thought was, Is this a joke? All at once I was relieved and shocked to find that the first person I told didn't freak out.

The experience gave me a lot of confidence. It helped me to realize that I was being too hard on myself.

Mr. Smith told me about the Hetrick-Martin Institute for Gay and Lesbian Youth. At HMI they had an afterschool center where I could meet other gay and lesbian teens. I couldn't believe that there were other people out there who were going through the same thing I was.

At Hetrick-Martin I got to know kids from all over the city, and of all races. It didn't matter that everyone was gay. What mattered was that everyone was cool. It was a place where I didn't have to hide who I was and where I could just be myself. At first I kind of felt uncomfortable being around other gay people. The trouble was that after pretending to be somebody else for so long I really didn't know who I was. The only thing I had thought about since I was 11 years old was what was I going to do about this gay sh-t. At 14, I didn't know how to think about anything else.

Then I found that I was not only gay, I also liked to have fun. I liked to go to the movies. I liked to hang out and chill with my friends, and I loved to listen to music. I was smart. I liked to do things that anybody else liked to do. I was a human being just like everybody else; I just happened to be gay. I didn't admit that to myself until I was 14.

It was around this time that I started my first relationship. His name was Chris. I met him at HMI and I found that I liked talking to him. We would hang out with our friends, go to clubs, or just chill and talk. I found that with Chris I felt happier than I had ever felt with any girl. Our relationship was totally based on friendship and respect.

Through all of this I was still cutting school and my mom would get suspicious about me hanging out late at night. Sometimes I would come home high on an acid tab and try to act as if I weren't high. I didn't care about school anymore. My only concerns became clubs, my friends, and hanging out. My mother finally got fed up. She told me I wouldn't amount to anything, that I would be a bum when I grew up. She kicked me out of my house and sent me to live with my father.

I hated my father's house. He put so many restrictions on me that I wasn't used to. I had to be home by 11:30 p.m. If I wasn't he would yell and scream and let me have it. I hated having to put up with that. And I was fed up with living a lie.

One day I arrived home and my father was sitting on the couch watching TV. It was a Friday night and it was only 10:30.

"Where were you?" my father yelled.

"I was out," I told him.

"What were you doing?"

By this point I was quite angry. I mean, who the f--k did this man think he was to be screaming on my time? I wasn't a little kid, and I was sick and tired of him telling me how to act, what to do, when to do it, and with whom. So I told him that it was none of his business where I was and that he should stay the hell out of my life. That got him very upset.

All of a sudden he grabbed me. "Goddammit, you're my son," he said, "and I want to know what you're doing." He started to cry and demanded I tell him if I was using drugs, if I had a girl-friend, a job? But the question that really hurt me was, "Are you a f--got?" It wasn't so much the question itself as the way he asked me. He had the most hateful look on his face, as if he were literally ready to kill someone.

"Let me get the f--k out of this house," I yelled. "I don't want to live here anymore."

"You're not leaving this house until you tell me what you're up to," he said.

"Let me go or I swear I'm going to jump out of that window," I replied. The only problem was that the window was five stories up, and I meant what I said.

He started to grab me and hit me. I was screaming and telling him that I was going to kill him. I was actually very scared. He kept telling me to shut up because the neighbors were listening. I told him I wanted them to hear. I wanted to kill him. I wanted to open the door and leave but he wouldn't let me.

My heart was beating fast and I was gasping for air and crying. I pushed him away, ran for the window, opened it, and was ready to jump, when my father grabbed me. He became very afraid for me, and he said that he was very sorry, and begged me to forgive him. I said that it was all right.

The next day was Saturday and my father called me from his job and told me in a really nice way that in the afternoon we were going to the doctor. I asked why. "You know, just to get a checkup," he said. Later in the day he came to pick me up. When we walked into the office the doctor asked me, "So what's the problem?"

"This ain't a doctor," I thought. "This is a therapist." I was upset that my father had lied to me and afraid that I would have to spend more time at the hospital. The doctor recommended to my father that I be admitted to Jacobi Hospital. Once I got there they took a lot of blood from me and then locked me up in a glass room with this man who smelled really bad and who kept talking to himself. Then they gave me this nasty food.

Later they made me talk to a social worker. He kept asking me what was wrong but I wouldn't tell him. I didn't tell him anything but he still felt that he had the right to tell my father that he thought I was gay. After a few hours I was sent to another hospital in the Bronx just for teens and then, after about a week, transferred back to the hospital I had been in when I was 12. My father and mother would talk to me about how much they loved me and how they would support me in anything I did.

I felt angry and confused because I had never told them anything or officially "come out" to them—someone else had. I felt bad that my parents had to go through all this. I knew they were sad and that they didn't want me to be gay. To be honest, if I had a choice I would not have chosen to be gay either. Who in the world would choose to go through all the name calling, all the bashings, and all the other sh-t gay people have to go through every day?

In a way I was glad that my parents found out while I was in the hospital because I didn't have to go through the "coming out" experience by myself. I had social workers and other people there for me. We would have family therapy where they would put my mother, father, and me with a social worker to talk about what life would be like for me when I left the hospital. It was agreed that I would go back to live with my mother, and a contract was drawn up about what the rules would be.

My parents and I would have heated arguments about what school I would go to and about my being gay. I told them it wasn't any of their business who I slept with. They disagreed and said I was just confused and that I would grow out of it. They would talk to me about AIDS, trying to scare me into not being gay. I told them that I already knew a lot about AIDS and ways to prevent getting it. They acted as if I was stupid, and didn't know anything. I would tell them about ways you can and cannot get it, and that if I had sex I would always use a condom no matter what the circumstances. I also told them that I was not sexually active, which was true. They acted as if I would get AIDS from the air just because I was gay. They were so ignorant in so many ways.

My mother and I would talk about what my being gay meant to our relationship. I explained to her that I was still the same person and that it didn't matter. My mother would tell me that she was upset because she was not going to have any grandchildren from me. That made me angry. "Who are you thinking about," I asked her, "you or me?"

After two months I left the hospital and went to live with my mother. I decided to go to the Harvey Milk School, a high school for gays, lesbians, and bisexuals, and things have gotten a lot better since then. I have plenty of friends and am happy with my life. Coming out to my family was hard but, now that I have, I can tell my parents almost anything and they give me all the support in the world.

I know now that I didn't really want to die. What I really wanted was to live in a world where I wouldn't have to deal with people's prejudices. Suicide is no way out. It's a permanent solution to a temporary problem. There's always another solution even when it seems like there isn't. For me, asking for help and coming out were two big steps toward learning to accept myself and not let other people's stereotypical perceptions of gay people put me down.

Racking, Bombing, Tagging ... My Career as a <u>Writer</u>

By Anonymous

The names and some of the details in this story have been changed.

When I was about 5 or 6 years old I used to love going shopping in Manhattan with my mom. I hated the shopping part. It was the subway ride I was interested in. I would always ask my mom if I could ride the Mickey Mouse train. I loved that train. It was beautifully painted, with huge colorful images of my favorite cartoon characters. I remember the Donkey Kong train, the Smurf train, and the train that had the naked lady with big breasts on it. In those days, whole subway cars were covered with amazingly detailed pictures that blended together with beautifully intricate writing. I had no idea who painted those pictures.

I started to find out when I was 9. I was playing ball in back of a school in my neighborhood when about nine or ten kids came into the schoolyard. Everyone else stopped what they were doing to see what was going to happen next. My boy Frankie, who was also known as Dash-Two because that's what he used to write on the walls around the neighborhood, approached one of them angrily

and proposed a fair fight—no boys involved, just one-on-one.
Frankie got the beating of his life that day. I didn't understand
what the whole fight was about, so I asked him. "He dissed my
sh-t," Frankie said. The kid he fought was Dash-One. He went on
to tell me that Dash-One had written over his tag on the walls and
on the trains. "The 5 line isn't big enough for two Dashes," he explained. Frankie wanted to be Dash-One, king of the 4 and the 5
trains. That's when I realized that graffiti was not just about
Mickey Mouse characters and huge colorful pieces of art.

One day in junior high I went over to Frankie's house and he
showed me a book of photographs of paintings he and his friends
had done on the trains. At last I saw the people behind these paintings. There were pictures of groups of kids in train yards and inside
trains and they all had smiles on their faces as if they were getting
away with something (which they were). By this time the Transit
Authority had a chemical that could wash off all of the paint or, if
they couldn't do that, they just wouldn't let the trains run with graffiti on them. I asked Frankie why he did it. All he said was "fame."

After that, I began to take a closer look at the writing around the
neighborhood. Slowly I began to understand it. I began to recognize "tags" that I'd seen before. Some of them belonged to people I
knew. When I turned 11, the older writers I knew gave me my own
tag, Ti-One. The way I wrote it was pitiful compared to what other
people were doing but I loved it. I used to write on the walls of
abandoned buildings. I never left the safety of my neighborhood.
Seeing my tag all over the neighborhood was great but what was
even better was one day in the seventh grade when some kid I
didn't even know came up to me and said, "I saw you up in Manhattan on a truck." Who knows how many other people saw it
wherever the truck went. I became a celebrity. Kids started calling
me by my tag. Older kids who were once sending me to buy them
sandwiches were giving me more respect, and I had not even left the
neighborhood yet. Meanwhile I was getting better at using paint.

I also became better at stealing. Before the "bomb" came the
"rack." No one ever bought paint. We always stole it—along
with just about anything else we could stuff down our pants.

Stealing became a way of life. So did fighting. My first graffiti-related fight was with this kid who wrote Voke-One. He lived in the neighborhood but he hung out in Manhattan. No one really liked him. His crew, KT (Krylon Team), and my crew, KDS (Kings Don't Stop) had a lot of beef, meaning we hated each other and fought every time we saw each other.

When I was with twenty or so other kids I would talk about how I wished Voke would come around the corner right now. I went over all of his stuff and his boys' stuff. Come to think of it, I didn't even know why I had beef with KT. I just saw their stuff and I went over it. My crew had beef; I had beef. That's all I knew. I was young and dumb. Little did I know that I would not always have them to protect me.

One day I was in the train station on my way to school when Voke and Sez and his brother Chaner came in. One of them saw a KDS tag on my bookbag and asked me what I wrote. I told them I didn't write. I was so scared I was stuttering. They knew I was lying. One of them hit me and they then proceeded to kick me when I was on the ground. People were in the station seeing all of this yet no one did a thing to stop it. I had to get six stitches in the backside of my head. After that, when I knew I would be alone I carried a lead pipe, and I would always watch my back.

The fights I would get in now and then didn't stop me from writing. During the summer before eighth grade I started leaving the neighborhood, going to the train yards and the lay-ups (the tracks where they keep trains during the weekend and at night). I loved writing on trains and, for a while, that was all I did. Some trains were getting buffed (cleaned) and some were slipping through with graff (writing) on them. I didn't really care. I just loved the tunnels, the yards, the lay-ups, and the occasional fame.

For a while I was king of the double Cs. They laid the trains up within a few blocks of my house and I'd hit them practically every day. I was 13 then, and I was hanging out with older kids and doing a lot of stealing. I snuck out almost every night and if I wasn't out writing, I was hanging out talking about it. But I always came home on time and played good with my parents.

They never knew anything about me except my grades, which were average. They were so blind.

But pretty soon bombing trains got boring. Most of the time, the trains would get cleaned up and the world never got to see my artistic masterpieces. My friends and I still hit Transit now and then but only to take pictures and, more importantly, to piss off the TA (Transit Authority). Then it started getting risky. The TA started leaving big, gaping holes in the fences to lure us in, and putting dogs in the train yards. Toys (amateurs) who got caught would sometimes exchange information about other, better-known writers to get themselves off. A friend of mine was picked up by the police at his house, arrested, and told to either pay the city $100,000 in damages or go to Spofford Juvenile Detention Center for six months. He got locked up.

After I heard that, I never told anyone my real name or where I lived. A lot of the time I didn't even tell kids I met for the first time that I wrote at all. I felt the TA was finding more and more ways to thwart us writers and it just wasn't worth going to jail. Once in a while we'd hit up trains, though, just to remind them that we were still there. One night me and a friend went to the R lay-ups at City Hall to do the insides of a train. We broke the window, went in, and started working. Five minutes later the doors opened up and in came the detectives. I spent twenty hours in a cage at Central Booking, six of them handcuffed to a bench. A kid in the cell happened to like my shirt and tried to take it. When I wouldn't let him have it he hit my friend. After that experience, I became a little disillusioned with writing and stopped—for a while.

A lot of my older friends who had gotten me into it had already stopped writing because they felt graffiti was dead (a few of them were on the road to being dead themselves), because of beef they had with other writers, or just because they were getting too old for it. Aside from the risks, it was also more of a hassle. We would have to go farther and farther out of the city to steal paint. There was a time when all I had to do was go to the Woolworth's on 14th Street. Now I would find myself in West Bumblef--k, Connecticut, hoping I hadn't come all that way for nothing.

I stopped writing for a month. That month all I talked about was writing. Finally, I got some paint and a friend and I walked down Flatbush Avenue hitting up gates and trucks and walls. It felt good to get back into the swing of things. Bombing on the streets was different, there were more things to do, to climb, and to write on. I started to hang out with kids my own age who wrote.

But writing on the street wasn't risk free either. That summer (ninth grade) my friends Nero and Dusk and I were doing a rooftop when police rolled up, surrounded the building, and came up to the roof. We tried to dip down the fire escape but a cop was waiting for us. They thought we were burglars and when they found out we were doing graffiti they laughed. They called us "Little f--king Picassos" all the way to the precinct where they called our moms and, after about four hours, let us go. I tried to make up some big lie about what happened but my parents didn't want to hear it.

Fortunately, the monthlong punishment they threatened me with didn't last a week and before I knew it I was writing again. I couldn't help it, I loved to go writing. It was like a sport; others would go to the courts to play ball, me and my friends would go writing. The difference was that on the court you were a basketball player and afterward you could be whatever you wanted to be. After the bomb you were still a writer; it followed you wherever you went. The beef followed you, your tag followed you, just the urge or the need to write followed you. I remember one time when I was out on Long Island at a family barbecue and I snuck away from the party, went into the garage, stole a can of paint, and went to the local schoolyard and did a huge outline. There was no graffiti around and I doubted anyone would see it but still the graff was in me wanting to come out.

I haven't been bombing in about a year. I'll write once in a while if someone hands me a can of paint but I get scared I'll get hooked again.

Even now, after catching all those stitches over graffiti-related beef, even after spending what seemed like a lifetime in Central Booking fighting for the clothes on my back, even after all of that, the graffiti is still dying to come out.

No More Clubbing for Me

By Fabayo McIntosh

Imagine it's about midnight and you've just stepped into your favorite club. The lights are flashing different colors and there are so many people. Everyone's either smoking or drinking. As you walk farther into the club and start hearing the music, you begin to get your groove on. You're a little annoyed at the high price ($30) you've just paid to get in, but you're ready to party. Then it happens—someone spoils your evening by offering you a drug like acid or wooze.

Whenever I go clubbing I get an adrenaline rush from the music and the dancing. But it seems like other clubgoers get high off of drugs that can burn through their skin. Like wooze, which is crack and marijuana rolled in a joint. Supposedly it makes you feel like you're in heaven and no other drug can match it—but I'll pass. I don't want anything to do with drugs, especially at a club. In my neighborhood I have seen many drug users. Most of them were decent people who decided that they just wanted to get high a couple of times and later down the road they got addicted. I don't want that to happen to me so I stay away from the madness.

But it's hard to avoid drugs when you're at a club. People you don't even know will come up to you and ask if you have any drugs and the generous ones offer you some—for free. Although I always say no, it seems like every other person in the club is smoking weed so I wind up catching contacts from them. My eyes get red and watery and I smell like smoke. Not a good picture when you get back home and your mother looks at you.

I don't appreciate the behavior of people who are on drugs either. I don't want to dance with someone who is high and drunk. They either act too forward or real stupid. If you don't want to dance with them they will get upset and say you're "not all that" or "Why you playing yourself?" Or they get too close and try to dance really slow to a fast song. Even if you do your best to avoid the drug users, they'll end up doing something that will affect you. In an overcrowded place like a dance club, drugs make people overreact and get out of control. Minor situations soon become major deals.

Once at the Tunnel, a guy who was dancing bumped into another guy. Since they both had been smoking weed and drinking, something as minor as this, which could have been resolved by saying "Excuse me," ended in a big fight that cleared the dance floor for a few minutes. Another night, I was standing on a block-long line to get into the Tunnel. Two guys started fighting and everybody got scared and started running. Girls were falling and getting trampled. Guys were taking advantage of the situation, digging pockets and trying to snatch earrings. A few people even had to go to the hospital. And the guys that were fighting were so high they probably didn't even realize they had started the whole conflict. My friends and I ran at first; then we moved to the side. Still, one of my friends ended up getting her wallet snatched.

I used to think these were a couple of isolated incidents, since I have only been to a few clubs—the Tunnel, Legend, and Golden Pavilion. But my friend says it's like that everywhere. I know that parties are like an open area where you feel free to do what you want to do. But there are limits. Freedom must balance itself with respect for everyone present at the party. And the carefree aroma that's in the clubs has got to go. If people have to smoke, clubs should have a smoking area and if they have to do heavy drugs then they should have a house party and invite their friends over. I paid my money just like the people who use drugs so why should I suffer?

From what I've seen, club owners have a lot to do with the problem: bouncers don't confiscate drugs so people feel free to bring them. Other than weapons, the only thing bouncers will take is alcohol and that's because they sell it inside for outrageously high prices. (A small cup of gin and juice—Snoop Doggy Dogg's favorite drink—costs $12 at some of the clubs I've been to!) I think club owners pretend they don't know about the drugs, but everyone knows that drugs and alcohol go hand in hand. So of course they'll make more money from the drug users.

What makes the situation worse is clubs don't generally card their customers. I think club owners just put up those signs (the ones that say you must be 18 to party and 21 to drink) to let the police think they're going by the book when they're really not. I've never been to a club that asked me for ID to get in or to buy a drink (I was 16 when I bought my first drink). Underage kids like myself and even younger get in, and they are the wildest. I've got sense but a lot of other kids don't. They are the ones who do most of the smoking and drinking. They feel that's how you can act "adult." I'm sorry, a 16-year-old is not adult enough to hang with 25-year-olds.

It's been less than a year since I joined the club scene but it's already fading away for me. Before, I would continue partying despite the drugs and the fights but enough is enough. I don't even have fun anymore. The thrill is gone. I'm just wasting my money. My idea of a good time is not getting high or catching contacts or getting rowdy or getting hurt. Clubbing is no longer fun for me—it's dangerous. My last party was the prom. These days my friends and I go over to each other's houses or to the movies or we sit at home with MTV. I know that doesn't sound like much but it beats being in a nasty environment.

Karate Killed the Monster in Me

By Robin K. Chan

I was fed up. From the time I was 4 years old, I was teased and pushed around by bullies on my way home from school because I was short and frail looking. My family and I also got harassed by racist punks because we were the only Asian people living in a White neighborhood.

These incidents grew the hate monster inside of me. Most days, I would come home from elementary school either angry or crying. My family and friends tried to comfort me, but I had been storing up the loads of anger inside for too long. I thought I was going to explode.

When I was about 9, I found the answer to my problems. I decided to learn karate so I could break the faces of all the people on my "hit list" (anyone who had ever bullied me or my family).

I started nagging my parents about learning karate. They agreed because they wanted me to build up my self-esteem, learn some discipline, and have more self-confidence. All I wanted was to learn the quickest way to break someone's neck, but I didn't tell that to my parents.

I was about 10 years old when I finally got my chance. My first dojo (that's what martial arts students call the place where they study and practice) was small, musky, and smelled lightly of sweat. The instructor, Mr. Sloan, was as strict as an army drill sergeant.

Mr. Sloan taught us how to do strange abdominal exercises that were like upside-down sit-ups and really difficult to do. He wouldn't allow any slacking off from people who got tired. It was only the first day, what did he want from us! I quickly discovered that I was really out of shape. Before the first lesson was over, I was already thinking about dropping out.

By the end of the second lesson, however, I had decided to stick with it. Mr. Sloan was teaching us cool techniques for breaking out of arm and wrist locks and that got me interested.

Mr. Sloan was a good instructor. Within a few months, my class of beginners went from learning the basic punch, block, and kick, to learning a flying jump kick. He also taught us effective techniques for breaking out of headlocks and strangleholds. We enhanced our skills by sparring with each other and practicing at home.

Although the dojo had limited resources (there were no boards to break, no martial art weapons, and no fighting gear), I still learned a lot and had a lot of fun. I became more flexible from the rigorous exercises. In addition to practicing our karate moves, we did push-ups, sit-ups, leg, arm, torso, and back stretches to limber up.

We also meditated together. Near the end of class, Mr. Sloan would "guide" us through the meditation by telling us to clear our minds. One time, he told us to picture ourselves breaking free of a barrier or knocking a barrel or a wall to pieces. He said that whenever we had problems or faced challenges that got us frustrated, we should go to a quiet place, relax, and close our eyes. In our minds, we should picture ourselves knocking over that problem or challenge. Mr. Sloan said that doing this should make us feel better. After meditating on "killing" the problem, he said, our minds would be clear and we'd be more determined to solve it.

Mr. Sloan also made it clear that he was teaching us karate not just so we'd be able to kick someone's ass real good, but so each of us could become a role model. A role model, he explained, was someone with a good conscience, good morals, self-respect, and respect for others.

We worked on developing these qualities in class by bowing to the instructor, addressing him as "sir" or "sensei," treating fellow students with respect, and listening to our sensei's lectures, which taught us about respect, discipline, manners, etc. We were taught to exercise these qualities not only in the dojo, but outside as well.

The goal of becoming a role model was a major factor in my wanting to continue to study karate. I no longer saw the martial arts as a way to get back at people who hurt me. I knew from experience that there were already enough menacing and evil people in this world. I didn't want to become one of them.

After a few months, I was much more self-confident and disciplined. I knew that I was now capable of protecting myself against enemies. Whether or not I chose to fight someone who bullied me was beside the point; I knew that I could knock them out. Just knowing that made me feel good about myself, so why fight when you're already ahead? Besides, not fighting would save my knuckles a lot of pain.

The insults and slurs I encountered did not bother me as much anymore. As a matter of fact, the discipline and basic philosophy I learned from karate held back the punches I was tempted to throw when people tried to provoke me to fight.

For example, one day when I was walking home from school, two teenage guys walked into me. One of them said, "Watch it, Ch-nk," and shoved me. They started pushing me but I just blocked their pathetic pushes. They weren't getting enough thrills from just shoving me, so they started cursing and spitting at me too.

I started getting really aggravated. Then I remembered something Mr. Sloan had told me when I asked him what to do when someone bothers you. "Low-lifes like these do not deserve the time and energy you put into punching them out," he said. "Just walk away and splash some cold water on your face."

I cooled down and started walking away. The two guys saw that I was not affected by their stupid remarks. I heard one of them say, "Forget that Ch-nk, man."

It was ironic how I wanted to learn karate so that I could beat up people like these, and then, when I got the chance, I didn't go through with it. What karate taught me was that fighting isn't the right way to solve a problem. It just turns you into one of those low-lifes who don't have the conscience, respect, manners, or education to know how to handle their problems any other way.

I was good enough at karate by that point that it wouldn't have been a fair fight. But if I had given in to the temptation to beat those guys up, I would have felt ashamed and guilty. I would have disappointed Mr. Sloan, who taught me that the most important rule of karate is not to fight unless it's necessary for self-defense; my parents, who told me never to fight with anyone even if they are wrong; and myself, because I feel that it is wrong to take advantage of a situation.

The time and effort I was putting into karate was getting me worthwhile results. I used to be wild when I was with my friends, but I had become more reserved and well-behaved. I also used to slack off in school but not anymore. I really started gearing up and hitting the books. My teachers and parents noticed the difference and were happy with what they saw.

I was even becoming a role model for some of my friends. They told me that they had never seen me work so hard before, and they admired the high grades I was earning in school. They decided to follow my example and started pulling their acts together and improving their own grades.

Unfortunately, Mr. Sloan's class ran for only a year and when time was up, all of us were really upset. But our instructor had a new class of misfits to turn into the fine role models we had become.

Studying karate was a wonderful experience. I'm thankful to my extraordinary and deserving instructor, Mr. Sloan, and to my great family who let me go to the dojo and have supported me always. Together, Mr. Sloan and my parents have made me realize that I should always try my best and put a sincere effort into whatever I do. They have geared me up, morally and spiritually, to reach for the stars.

A Bull's-Eye on My Body

The Culture of Sexual Assault

Tired of Being a Target

By Loretta Chan

On August 3, 1993, at 3:30 p.m., some jerk threw a Snapple bottle at me while I was crossing a Manhattan street. I don't know what provoked him—I didn't even know who he was.

When I turned back from the curb where the bottle had landed (thank God it didn't hit me), all I saw was a group of guys standing around, smiling, and saying, "Look at her, look at her." When I turned back in the direction I was originally heading, a guy said to me, like it was funny or something, "Baby, somebody doesn't like you."

And I just continued walking to the train station like nothing had happened. At least I acted like nothing had happened. But, behind my sunglasses, I was trying hard not to cry.

I had never felt so defenseless against anyone. It caught me off guard and I couldn't do anything to protect myself or to retaliate. For that moment, I wasn't the I-am-woman-hear-me-roar girl that a lot of people know me as. Instead, I became one of those pitiful girls who can't stand up against a male chauvinist pig. I had never walked away from a situation like that before without at least giving the guy a cold stare and letting him know that I was offended. But all I did this time was walk away like I couldn't care less about how I was treated.

I was on my way to a job interview and all I could think about was whether this incident was going to make me late. When I finally got to the train station, a lady told me that my leg was bleeding and handed me some tweezers. A piece of glass had gotten stuck in my leg when the bottle crashed into the curb. Great, I thought, now my interviewer would not only see that my eyes were red, but I would also be bleeding all over his office.

Trying to get the damn glass out of my leg made me half an hour late for my interview. Still, my main concern was whether or not I would get the job, not why some man I didn't know decided to throw a bottle at me.

Well, I got the job, but I couldn't get the Snapple bottle incident out of my mind. At home that night I told my mother about what happened. I was expecting her to comfort me.

Instead, she barely even looked up from her desk. The first thing she said to me, in her Chinese accent, was, "Because of what you wearing. It's too sexy." She even used the same hand gesture she uses when she yells at me for coming home late. She never even said that she felt bad about what had happened. No "Poor baby. Are you okay? Let me get you some milk and cookies." And for the next week, she inspected the way I dressed even more closely than before.

By now, you're probably wondering what I was wearing that day. It was a long, sleeveless floral dress that was almost down to my ankles. Okay, it was a little fitted, and had a slit on the side, but in no sense was it "slutty" or "showy" in comparison to what a lot of other girls were wearing on that hot day.

And what difference does it make? No matter what I was wearing, why should my mother blame me for getting a bottle thrown at me? He was the one who attacked me. Why did I always have to feel like I was on the defensive whenever I stepped out of the house?

Long before this, I'd learned how to stare straight ahead when passing any male and to walk very quickly. And the other basic stuff: to never get into an empty elevator alone with a guy and not to walk alone in a deserted area at night. But I never thought that anybody would ever attack me on the street, in broad daylight, as long as I minded my own business.

My mind became filled with hateful, violent thoughts about men. I remembered the times those a--holes had whipped out their penises on the train in front of me and started masturbating. I thought of the remarks from strangers on the street about my body. I thought about the perverts whispering their sexual fantasies to me as they passed me or were walking behind me. I had dealt with those things by just putting them out of my mind. But I couldn't forget the Snapple incident. As the disgruntled say, "I'm mad as hell and I'm not going to take it anymore."

So I started considering other options. First I thought of different ways of cursing guys out. Then I went down to the store to get a bottle of pepper spray. A week later I was looking at stun guns on 42nd Street. And for a moment I considered getting a small handgun and going to a shooting range to learn how to use it.

I wondered what would have happened to Mr. Snapple if I had something with me that day? I don't think I would have attacked him, especially if he was with a group of friends. But maybe I would have had the guts to curse the hell out of him, knowing that I was armed. Then again, maybe not. If he had thrown a bottle at me just because I was there, what would he have done if I really provoked him by fighting back?

As a result of the Snapple incident, I've come to believe something that I've always denied—that women are, in general, more vulnerable than men. Though men have to be on guard for danger wherever they go, they still have a sense of security knowing that they might be a match for another male. Plus, they aren't attacked as often as females are. We simply make easier targets—we might as well have bull's-eyes emblazoned on our bodies.

And we are constantly reminded that we are in danger: people warn us that we shouldn't be taking the train at night alone or at all, that we shouldn't be walking down a deserted street after dusk, that there are certain areas a young lady should never wander through. However, men can roam the entire earth with minimal caution.

What really kills me is that I'm back to square one. I hate spending all this time bitching about something that half of our population has to put up with and not have a solution. It would be too cheesy to just end with a moral for the males like: "Have respect for women." It's such a simple rule of thumb, yet they've had difficulty with it for centuries.

It would be even worse for me to tell other women that we'll just have to put up with abuse and harassment for the rest of our lives. I refuse to accept as a fact of life that males are going to continue treating women this way. Just the thought that women in the future, maybe my own daughters, will be treated as second-class humans makes me want to shred every male on this planet to pieces. In this moment of passion and fury, that's the only solution I can seem to conjure up.

I also know I'm probably not going to physically attack the next man who pinches my butt or makes a lewd comment. So what else can be done? Maybe it begins with a lecture to a dirty old man on the street about how you didn't appreciate the crude remark he just made. Yes, it takes guts. It'll take even more guts to work up from the dirty old man to the construction worker or the group of hoods on the corner. And unfortunately, there will be times when you'll just have to use your common sense and hold back from spitting fire because of what might happen afterward.

It's driving me crazy that I don't have a better solution to this problem, especially since I know I'm going to be facing it again in just a couple of minutes, when I go outside. Because as far as those dirty old (and young) men out there are concerned, I've still got a bull's-eye emblazoned on my body.

Why Guys Talk Nasty

By Nanci S. Paltrowitz

Catcalls. We hear them all the time. Whether we're walking down the street or riding the subways. "Hey baby, you got it goin' on!" "Your ass is phat!" or "What's up with you and me?"

Ever wonder why guys yell out these things about a woman's body? Is it that they want to look cool? Do they think that women like it? Or is it just because they have nothing better to do?

I asked several guys and some of their answers were enough to make my skin crawl. "Sometimes you just want to see their reaction," said Sinohe Terrero, 18, of Humanities High School. "You just test them to see how good they think they look."

I asked Sinohe to tell me the kinds of things he says. "If she got big tits," he explained, he'll say, "let me throw something on them and lick them to the last drop!" Is this right? Is it harassment or just plain fun?

According to Sinohe, talking this way can't really be considered harassment because he doesn't do it "constantly," just once in a while. Sinohe doesn't think his comments are all that bad. "I try to keep it low; I have a friend that throws bottles at them.

"They should be happy," he continued. "At least you're payin' attention to them." But even if they were happy, girls are certainly not paying attention back. Every one of the guys that I interviewed said that the girls usually ignore the comments they or their friends make.

"They just put their hands up," said Jonathan Ortiz, 14, also of Humanities High School. "They don't bother."

When that happens the guys don't always just walk away. They often respond with things like "B--ch," "Sl-t," or "H-." According to Frank Morales (not his real name), 24, "Sometimes they [even] try to grab the girl's arm."

In spite of being ignored, Sinohe still insists that a lot of women seem to like it. "Some women, if you say that they have a nice butt, they'll change the way they walk," he claimed.

Maybe men are somehow getting a mixed message. Maybe there are a few girls who smile when these comments are made or others who yell back comments about the male anatomy, but this is only a tiny minority. I have heard more stories of girls slapping guys in the face.

Peter Anthony Collado, 23, even told me about one girl who brought a group of guys to beat up the people that were saying these things to her.

"[Women] don't really like it," said Alex Yablakov, 17, of John Dewey High School. "If a girl has any respect for herself, she wouldn't like it. I wouldn't like it."

Even Sinohe admitted that making crude remarks can make life miserable for someone. "I knew a girl once who was afraid to go out of her house because old men would be harassing her," he said.

So if girls don't like these comments, if they ignore them and keep away from the people who make them, what makes some guys continue to do it?

Many of the ones I spoke to feel that it's peer pressure. "It makes me look good in front of my friends," says Richard Santana, 18, of Humanities High School. Frank Morales agrees, saying that although he himself doesn't do it, he knows plenty of people who do—"the whole block," in fact. "Sometimes they want to show off," he said.

Damien Estevez (not his real name), 17, also of Humanities High School, admitted that he does it more when he's with his friends, "because I got more support. They can back me up."

Not all guys do it, though. There is a group that doesn't agree with the catcall routine. "It makes [guys] look stupid. Most of my friends that say those things, I never seen them with a girl," explained Jonathan. Alex agrees. "It's not a good line like some people think," he says.

I asked these guys how they'd feel if it were their sister or mother who were being yelled at and they all said that they'd feel disrespected. Sinohe told me about a time when he and his mother were walking down the street together and several guys started to yell things out to her. "When they yelled at my mother, I felt insulted!" he said.

Although this has never happened to Peter, he says that he would feel disturbed if it did. "I'd probably turn around and start cursing them out," he told me.

So if these guys feel insulted and disrespected when others yell out these comments, then why do they still do it?

The truth is, they don't feel that they are doing anything wrong. They are merely expressing themselves in the only way that they know how. "You can't break tradition," explained Sinohe.

But Alex disagrees. "There's better ways of expressing yourself," he said. "I've never seen people get far with it."

Tell Him Why

By Lisa Frederick

Excuse me, do I know you? Do you know me?
Yes, I do know you. You're the brother hanging on the
    corner with nothing to do
Now you have nerve telling me about myself
When you have empty pockets on the right and emptier
    pockets on the left
Just because I ignore your hisses, ain't no need for
    disses
I'll treat you like a mister if you treat me like a missus
I'm telling you this cause I'm sick and tired
There's a difference between being heckled and being
    admired
You know what I'm talking about, you do it every day
You want the attention so be attentive to what you say
It's lewd, it's crude, it's downright rude
But in your head you're thinking, "What the heck"

And when a sista walks by, you give her no respect
I'm a young female and I'm Black too
And in this day and age, that's two strikes against you
So don't give me no stress because you fail to impress
If my own people give me nothing, others will give me
    still less
Give us what we deserve: a lot of respect, a lot of love
Cause you know I'm right when I say you need us
When you entered this world, it was a woman you saw
    first
Behind every good man stands a better woman
So give us what we ask, ain't no big task
And if you fall off the track we'll be there to pick up
    the slack
With us you won't lack, cause sista's got your back
But I can't help you up if you only bring me down... I
    won't stick around
I can't help you if you won't help yourself, so get those
    want ads off the shelf
Don't get me wrong, honey, it's not all about the money
Whoever said life was a joke won't find this funny:
Think you look cute with a beeper and a Malcolm X hat
But I don't think Malcolm would speak to a sista like
    that
He would know that we're dignified, full of pride, clas-
    sified, bona fide and refined
He would've also stated that we're educated, compli-
    cated, understated, underrated, and underestimated
Unashamed, unclaimed, untamed, unchanged, under-
    standing, undemanding... but still disrespected
We're used, bruised, and left confused
So... my brown-bag-drinking, big-mouth-bragging,
    1,000-gold-chain-wearing, imaginary-BMW-
    driving, Jafarian-belt-hoopin', bead-wearing,
    Rastafarian-talking, wannabe-down-with-
    culture brother

(you know it's true, at least one applies to you)
When you see us walking by and you say "hi"
Don't get mad cause we don't reply
It's just something in our culture that we miss
I know Isis and Nefertiti weren't spoken to like this
Oh, you don't see our crowns but we did come down
      from a nation of queens and kings
Just think of us as royalty in jeans
A lot of love you can expect
If you just give your sista her respect.

The Price of Love

Boys, Girls, and Violence

Letters to Parents

Dear Mom,

I'm writing you this letter to let you know how I feel. I feel anger, hatred, and rage. I also feel self-pity, shame, and sadness.

Last summer something happened to me that was so terrible I have trouble writing it. A day that was supposed to be festive and happy turned into a nightmare that will last for the rest of my life.

On July 4th, I was raped by two "friends" in the backseat of their car. I met them at my friend's barbecue. One of them went to my school. I feel totally used and betrayed. No matter how I try to convince myself, I still think it's my fault. I offered to let them drive me home.

I'm sorry, Mom. Sorry I didn't report it to the police, and even more sorry that I didn't talk to you. Doing so would have helped me deal with the pain. Your support and understanding would have made this period in my life more healing.

Latoya (name changed)

Dear Grandma,

I need to talk to someone because I need to get something off my chest. I know you told me if anybody put their hands on me I would have to handle my business. And yes, I'm scared of him.

You always told me if I could avoid fighting I should do so. So rather than try to hit him back, I asked him to tell me the purpose of hitting me. He said I got him upset because of something I did to him, that hitting me was his way of expressing his feelings of hurt and anger.

I told him that I understood that he was mad at me but that hitting me does not make matters better. I told him that putting his hand on me is pushing me away from him, and makes me not want to see or be with him anymore.

We're trying to communicate and work things out, but I guess I just wanted you to know what was going on in case things get really out of hand. I don't mean to worry you or upset you, and I hope you understand how hard it is for me to tell you all of this. I just need to get through this and be all right.

Cindy (name changed)

I Paid a High Price for Love

By Melissa Krolewski

The names and some of the details in this story have been changed.

I was standing on the lunch line at my junior high school one day when I felt someone tug on my ponytail. When I looked behind me, a small guy with curly blond hair was smiling slyly. I turned to my best friend and giggled. Then he did it again. I thought it was the cutest thing in the world. After we got our lunch, he sat at my table, but didn't say a word.

In French class, my friend Julie informed me that the guy with no vocal cords was named Danny, he was 15, and he wanted to go out with me. "I don't even know the guy," I said with a laugh. Julie smiled and said, "Look, just get to know him. If you don't like him, you can dump him."

Danny followed me around to all my classes for the rest of the day but he didn't speak to me until after school, when he asked if he could walk me home. I told him he could. On the way, we stopped at the park and hung out for a while. We talked about our families, school, and music. Danny had a sense of humor and

made me laugh a lot. He seemed like a sweet guy. He was interested in everything I talked about and that made me feel special.
I decided to go out with him. After all, what could I possibly
lose?

I began spending time with Danny every day. We went to
school together and hung out afterward. He never failed to walk
me all the way home. I felt like I could depend on him and I
needed someone to depend on.

Before meeting Danny, I was never happy with my life. My
mother was forever putting down everything I did, making me
feel worthless. I was yearning for someone to really love me and
Danny became that person. I could talk to him about my problems at home, about how my mother and I never got along. He
would hold me when I was feeling down and promise that whatever happened, he'd be there. Safe and secure, I clung to Danny.
I thought I'd found my savior. It took me a long time to find out
I was wrong about him.

One day, about three months into our relationship, I was
wearing a bodysuit that I had just bought. When Danny saw me,
he said, "You're *my* girl. Why do you want to wear that and
show everyone what you have? Do you want to look like a
slut?" He handed me his hooded sweater and said, "Put this on
and zipper it." He made me feel ashamed of how I was dressed,
even though everyone was wearing bodysuits at the time.

I put on the sweater and zipped it partway up. Danny wasn't
satisfied; he zipped it up to my neck. He looked me in the eyes
and said, "I'm going to check on you, so don't even think about
taking it off." I thought this was his way of showing affection. I
thought it was so cute. After that, Danny was constantly telling
me what I could and couldn't do. I couldn't wear makeup, skirts,
or anything that he considered "slutty." I couldn't listen to
R.E.M. because he thought they played "devil music." I couldn't
go to the store. I couldn't even hang out with my two best
friends, whom I cherished. Danny started cutting all his classes
so that he could "check on me" and make sure I was doing what
he said.

At first, I didn't even notice how much Danny was controlling me. Love is blind and Danny was my first love. With him by my side, I was able to ignore my problems at home. As long as he was there, I was all right. In other words, I desperately needed him to cope with my own life. But soon my own life vanished. I needed him there so badly, I let him change the things about me that made me an individual. I was becoming a clone of Danny. I thought what he thought; I did what he did.

Danny justified giving me orders by making it clear that I was his property. "You're my girl," he kept telling me. And because I was his girl, I was supposed to listen to whatever he said. I didn't question this because I thought I'd be lost without him. I believed everything he told me, like, "I'm the only guy who'll take your sh-t." All I needed was for him to hold me. As long as his arms were tightly around me, I got what I wanted out of the relationship.

If I didn't do what he said, Danny would get angry—not just annoyed, but violently angry. As much as I hated admitting it, I was scared. I knew Danny had a short fuse and I didn't want to set it off. I was afraid of his temper but I was also afraid of losing him. So I obeyed him when he told me what to wear, to ignore all my friends, and to stay home if he wasn't with me.

As far as my friends were concerned, I had dumped them for Danny. They thought I was just being a b--ch and I don't blame them. I didn't give them any reason not to hate me. I never told them how trapped I was feeling, how vulnerable. In a sick way, I wanted to be trapped because it made me feel secure.

One day, about a year after I started going out with Danny, he wanted me to walk to his house (which was about a mile and a half away). It was a freezing cold day when there were about four inches of snow on the ground and I said no. That was the first time I didn't do what he said. Danny gripped my arm, twisted it to where it was painful, and pulled me. We were standing outside in my neighborhood and some people were out shoveling their sidewalks. I said no again in a firm tone, but low enough so that no one else could hear me. He twisted my arm more. With his other hand, he grabbed some of my hair and yanked me forward. Tears were forming in my eyes. I realized that the more I resisted, the more hurt I'd get and the more the neighbors would notice, so I tramped through the snow to his house.

I figured that once we got there, he'd leave me alone since he'd gotten his way. I was wrong. I didn't even have a chance to get my coat off before he punched me. Danny hit me everywhere except my face (knowing that would leave visible marks). He did slap my face once, though, which demeaned me completely. Then Danny shoved me into a chair and forced off my shoes.

I began crying hysterically. The only person who cared for me (or so I believed) was treating me like I was nothing. Danny tossed my shoes on the top of a cupboard where I couldn't get to them. "Shut the f--k up," he said. "Take your coat off, you ain't goin' nowhere." I just sat there sobbing. After about an hour of giving me dirty looks, Danny started to feel bad and apologized for everything. "I just wanted to be with you," he said. We made up. A couple of hours later, he got me my shoes and I went home like nothing had happened.

That type of incident became an everyday thing. I never said anything to anyone because I thought I deserved it. And I figured that having Danny hit me was simply the price I had to pay for having him hold me. I became more and more isolated. Danny would only let me see my friends when he was there. Since he had no problem hitting me in public and I didn't want my friends to see that, I avoided them. I was too depressed to even talk to them about what was happening. I knew they would feel bad for me and try to get me to leave him. Although I wanted to, I was too frightened of having to cope with the dread of being alone.

I did threaten to leave Danny a few times. His response was, "You can't get anyone else. Who would want you?" I believed him. I just accepted the low place I was in as my fate. This was all I thought I could ever amount to. I figured I would end up marrying him, dropping out of school, and becoming a lonely, beaten-up housewife.

Things continued to get worse between us. One day, I was in the bathroom at Danny's house, combing my hair, getting ready to go out. I could hear him telling his sister and his cousin about a fight we had at a party. He had dragged me down a flight of stairs because I wanted to ask someone something. He had caused a commotion and a friend's parent had to drive me home so I could get away from him. Danny told his sister he had done what he did because I was a b--ch.

"You're such a liar!" I yelled.

Danny stormed into the bathroom and pushed me hard enough to make me fall. I almost banged my skull on the bathtub. His sister started screaming, "I'm telling Mommy. I'm callin' the cops!" Then his mom came in with a bat, and started swinging it at him. She turned to me and said, "Don't worry, I'm sending him to live with his father." Danny ran out.

I was so incredibly embarrassed. I wouldn't have cared if he killed me, but why did he have to do it in front of everyone? Danny's cousin was crying. She begged me to leave him. "He'll never change," she said. The cops arrived but Danny was nowhere in sight. His whole family was out in the hall and I had to walk past them to leave the house. They all stared at me with pity. The police drove me home. This was the worst of all the times Danny hurt me because his entire family and the cops were involved. Everyone knew what was going on. Everyone wanted to protect me from Danny, when I thought Danny was my only protection.

For about four days after that, I tried to stay away from him. He would call me up and come to my house crying. I tried ignoring the phone calls and the doorbell ringing. I wanted badly to go out and see my friends, but when I did, Danny was there, a puppy-dog look on his face. "I'll change," he said. "I promise. I'm sorry." I gave in . . . again. I still believed Danny loved me. He will change, I thought. But it was more like a hope. Sometimes hope just isn't enough. He never changed. He only got worse. I took his abusive treatment for another five months, until his mother finally sent him away to live with his father. At last, I was free.

I was lucky. I didn't have to break up with him. His mom took care of the dirty work. Looking back, I blame myself for what happened. I should have stopped the vicious cycle sooner. I guess I was just terrified of being alone again. I was stuck in a bottomless pit of self-pity. Not even a slap in the face could wake me up . . . and I mean that literally.

For the first few months after Danny left, I didn't care what happened to me. I reunited with my friends but pretty much all we did was party. Then I met Greg. Neither of us was ready to jump into a committed relationship at first, so basically we became wonderful friends. Greg made me realize that Danny wasn't the only person who could care for me. Greg not only cared; he supported me in a positive way. He insisted that I deserved a lot more than what I had. Greg somehow made me see that I had the power to accomplish anything. We started going out and have been together for two years now.

Writing this story has been the final healing phase for me. I am now a completely different person than I was when I was with Danny. Although it was a horrible experience, at least I learned a lesson from my relationship with him: The worst thing you can do to yourself is to depend completely on someone else. I will never do that again and I will never let anyone else control, abuse, or hurt me in any way. I know now that you don't have to put up with that kind of treatment in order to be loved.

He Won't Stop Hitting Me

By Anonymous

The names in this story have been changed.

Rahim and I had only been together four months when he beat me up the first time. We had gone over to his house after school. He went outside and took an hour to come back. I got mad and decided I would write a fake letter to my friend Todd and let Rahim find it so he would get jealous. Later on that evening he found the letter, asked me who Todd was, and proceeded to punch me in the face, giving me a black eye. When I tried to hit him back he gave me a bloody nose. After that, of course I wanted to go home, but he wouldn't let me. He apologized and had the nerve to want to make love. I was foolish enough to let him.

Rahim didn't let me go home that night. The next day I went to school with a black eye and swollen nose. I had to lie to my friends and parents. I told one friend the truth and she told me to leave him. I got mad because that wasn't what I wanted to hear. To this day I regret ever telling her.

Rahim has been hitting me on and off for over a year now. He's hit me outside, in front of my friends, on the train, even in front of his own mother! Never in my house—yet. He's left marks on me twice: that first time and another time when he gave me a swollen jaw. Sometimes I hit him first but he really overdoes it. When he gets mad he's just a completely different person. He always says he'll change but he never does. The first few times I believed him, but not anymore. We went to a therapist once about six months ago but it didn't last.

I guess I stay with him because he does things that other boys wouldn't do. If I tell him to pick me up from somewhere he'll come. He'll give me everything. Everything! But that's not enough, because he doesn't respect me. He even cheated on me last summer. It took him a while to tell me the truth, but eventually he did. I was very hurt and I lied to him and told him I was cheating too. He wanted to hit me, but that time he didn't.

Another time I found a picture of him with his ex-girl and I told him it was over. Rahim wanted me to go with him to the girl's house and ask her if they were seeing each other again. I thought that he was crazy. So he locked me in his house so he could bring her to me. He wanted her to tell me that they weren't seeing each other anymore. She wouldn't come so he smacked her. I know because my friend Ricky lives in the same housing project as his ex-girlfriend and Rahim has a lot of friends down there.

I feel like such a coward when he hits me. I feel as though I can't win. I've had fights with many people and was not scared to hit them back. But I am scared to hit him back.

He thinks I can forget when he hits me, because he forgets when I hit him, but I don't hurt him as bad. We are both violent, but he's ridiculous and I'm frightened. Why do I love this guy so much? Why can't I leave him? Even if I wanted to it would be hard. He might not let me.

I wish I could tell my parents but I just can't. I'm not from a dysfunctional home or anything. I just wish I could get some help and that he could too. He really wants to change. I wish I knew about special counseling groups both of us could attend.

Most people do not discuss physical abuse among teenagers, but it happens to a lot of us. Some worse than others.

Dream Guy, Nightmare Experience

By Anonymous

The names in this story have been changed.

I'm lying on the floor, in a dark room, unable to move. Then I see him, standing over me, laughing. I try to move, but I'm paralyzed. He gets closer and closer and right when he's about to kiss me, I wake up, screaming. After that I'm too upset to go back to sleep, so I sit up and cry all night.

My nightmares aren't as vivid as before, but they're there. Just when I think it's finally over, the memories come back to haunt me. I keep thinking that maybe I could have done something to prevent it. Maybe if I hadn't been such a sucker for a happy ending. Maybe if I had thought ahead. Maybe . . . Maybe . . .

We didn't go to the same school but he lived in the neighborhood and was always hanging around. I used to see him in the morning before school. He was about 16, kind of tall, with short, dark hair and the most beautiful gray eyes I've ever seen. He'd say hi when he saw me and even though I didn't really know him, I started to like him. Occasionally, I'd stop and talk to him—nothing too personal. We talked about the movies we'd seen, music and stuff like that. I began to look forward to our little talks, and was disappointed when I didn't see him around the school. I was 13 at the time.

One day after school, he was waiting for me. I was with my friend Charlene. We were talking outside the school and I pretended that I didn't see him. He kept trying to get my attention, but I pretended not to notice. I don't know why—maybe I didn't want Charlene to know I had a crush on him.

When I said good-bye to my friend, I walked slowly to the end of the block.

"Hello," he called out to me.

I turned, slowly, and smiled at him. "Hi, Eric," I said shyly.

"Where are you going?" he asked.

I told him I was going to the train station. He asked if he could walk me there, and, being the lovesick puppy that I was, I said, "Sure." He carried my books and we talked. When we arrived at the station, he asked if he could have my phone number. I was so excited that I gave it to him without any hesitation.

He called that night. We talked for at least two hours. He told me that he lived with his aunt and his brother. He said he'd been wanting to talk to me for a while, that he liked me and wanted to get together sometime. That phone call made me the happiest person in the world. After I got off the phone with him, I called some of my friends and told them. Being liked by a guy made me feel important.

The next time I saw him, he walked me to the train station again, and we talked some more. Then he kissed me good-bye. It was just a small kiss, but it made me feel wonderful. I was convinced he was a great guy.

He called me again that night. We talked for a while, and just as I hoped, he "popped the question."

"Yes! I'll go out with you!" I half screamed. For the rest of the night, I was practically floating in midair, I was so happy. "Somebody loves me," I thought.

We were "boyfriend and girlfriend" for a grand total of five days. He called me and we saw each other throughout the week. Then after school on Friday, he was waiting for me in our usual meeting place, on the corner by the schoolyard. He said he wanted to take me someplace special that afternoon. I was thrilled. I thought maybe we would go to the movies or something. "But first," he said, "we have to stop by my house for a minute."

It was a pretty big apartment, but it looked like it hadn't been cleaned in years. He brought me into the kitchen and got a glass of water. Then we went into the living room and sat on a sofa with the stuffing coming out of it. He told me to leave my books on the floor. Then he turned on the television and shut off all the lights and said, "We'll go in a minute. I'm tired. I want to rest for a second. Sit down with me." So, I did.

We sat in the darkness and watched TV for a while. I asked him where his aunt and his brother were. He stared at me with those eyes and replied, "out," plain and simple. He was acting kind of weird, but I didn't want to say anything, because I thought he might get mad or something. He took my hand and started to kiss me. At first it was kind of nice. But then he started getting too aggressive, putting his hands in places they didn't belong.

I remember thinking to myself, "This doesn't feel right. What's he doing?" I started getting scared and told him to stop. But he didn't. I tried pushing him away, but I was too small. He was a lot bigger than me. He forced himself on top of me and pulled my pants down. No matter how much I struggled, he wouldn't let up. He held me down by the shoulders and raped me. I was crying and screaming, "No! Stop! Please stop!" But he wouldn't. Exhausted from crying and trying to get him off me, I stared into the blackness, tears sliding off of my cheeks.

It all happened very fast. As soon as I could, I fixed my pants, tried to wipe the tears away, and got the hell out of there. I walked the eight blocks to the train station and waited for the train in a daze. I kept telling myself that it didn't really happen, that it couldn't really happen—not to me.

On the train this guy pressed up against me and tried to talk to me. I just turned around and walked through to the other car. Then I caught this girl looking at me, like she knew. I gave her a really ugly stare and she looked away, embarrassed.

When I finally made it home, the first thing I did was jump in the shower. I washed my entire body, but I just couldn't seem to feel clean. I dried myself off and put on some clean clothes. Then I looked at the clothes I was wearing at the time it happened. I noticed blood on my pants and shirt. I had a small cut on my chest and my legs were scraped up—I guess from struggling. I took the clothes, balled them up, and put them in a plastic bag. I carried them to the incinerator and threw them out. Then I went into my room, lay down on my bed, and cried. Thank God my mother wasn't home.

I didn't want to think about it, but I couldn't help it. I'll never forget the look he gave me afterward. It was like he was proud of what he had done. Then something else popped into my mind: What if I get pregnant? I closed my eyes and tried to block the thought. (Thankfully, I wasn't, but I was really scared for a while.)

I saw him once more afterward when I went to the store with Charlene one day after school. I was getting some juice and, while I was walking up to the counter to pay for it, he and two of his friends came into the store. My heart raced and I dropped the bottle. It smashed on the floor, but I didn't hear it. Charlene grabbed me and pulled me out of there. She knew something was wrong, but she kept her mouth shut. I didn't leave my house for a few weeks after that. I was afraid I might see him again. I was staying home more and more. Playing sick seemed to be the only escape.

One day, my best friend was over at my house, and I decided to tell her. I just couldn't keep this horrible secret inside of me any longer. "Kate, I need to tell you something," I said. I took a deep breath and sat down. I tried to go slowly, but the words raced out of my mouth. "I was going out with this guy and I thought he was really nice but he wasn't. Kate, you're my best friend and I want you to help me. I was raped."

Kate just stared at me, in shock. Then the expression on her face changed to one of disbelief. "Well," she said, "how do you know if he really raped you?" I couldn't believe it. My best friend, doubting me, almost accusing me of lying. Things between us were never the same from then on. I can't say that I hate her, because I don't. I just don't talk to her—about anything.

Eventually, I told some other friends and a few adults. I am happy to say that all of them really helped me. They always listened when I needed to talk, anytime. Even if it was 3:30 in the morning and I had trouble sleeping, I could call them up and they'd help me get through it. Now I really regret not speaking to anyone sooner.

It happened almost three years ago, but I still think about it as though it were yesterday. I have to stop asking myself if it was my fault, if I "asked for it." It wasn't my fault, I didn't ask for it. I had no control over the situation. The only thing I did wrong was wait so long to get help.

Rape is a horrible thing, I know that now. You have to be aware. You have to be careful. It can happen to anyone. And yes, you can be raped by someone you know. One minute you're watching TV, riding along in a car, getting help with homework. The next minute you're fighting to get away, gasping for breath, staring off into the blackness. If it does happen to you, remember, it's not your fault. Tell someone fast. Get help. It'll really make a difference later on.

My Love, My Friend, My Enemy

By Anonymous

The names and some of the details in this story have been changed.

One afternoon, about two years ago, I was at the gym working out with a friend and I saw this really hot guy. He was a tall, slim, clean-cut kind of guy. He gave me this deep, penetrating look. A few days later I went back to the gym and saw him again. We started talking and it turned out he lived in my neighborhood. His name was Maurice. We started seeing each other and eventually started to go out.

He was just perfect for me. He was romantic and sweet and made me feel so secure. I remember one breezy night, late in the summer, we were walking around the neighborhood. He stopped to lean on a car, held my hands, and kissed me. He told me he really cared about me. I felt so good. My body tingled, and my soul was floating. I had finally found a real guy who wouldn't be afraid to make a fool of himself over me.

For the next four months we laughed and shared some really good times. We used to go to the movies to watch Disney cartoons. I got to know his family really well. He met mine too and they were crazy about him. I used to go to his house after school practically every day and play around with his little sister. His mom was a sweetheart. His dad was funny, and his older sister—well, I loved her. She treated me like I was a real part of the family. On my birthday she brought me flowers. Even after Maurice and I broke up, she called to wish me and my family a Merry Christmas.

People warned me that Maurice was a liar and that he would break my heart. I remember my friend Calvin and even my next door neighbor, Lydia, telling me not to go with him. I just thought Calvin was jealous because he liked me, and Lydia, well, she thought she knew it all. At that time I was so happy I couldn't imagine ever getting hurt.

When school started, Maurice stayed in Brooklyn and I started going to a new school in Manhattan. I had to adjust to a new lifestyle and make friends all over again. I changed the way I dressed, and even the way I acted. Where once I had been sweet and gentle all the time, I started acting bolder, tougher, and more assertive. Maurice just wouldn't understand. All he wanted was the sweet, innocent little girl he had once known. So we started arguing and arguing. I loved Maurice, but at the same time, I found myself falling for Franco, a guy at my new school. It was one of the hardest things I ever had to do, but I told Maurice I wanted to break up and why. He was furious. We didn't speak for weeks.

One day he called and we talked, and we started seeing each other again, but only as friends. He was a good friend. I felt even closer to him than when we were going out. Every time I broke up with my boyfriend, I'd always run to Maurice for support. I could even call him up for advice in the middle of the night. When Franco and I broke up, Maurice and I ended up trying to get back together, but it didn't work out. I guess we were both too immature and stubborn.

One afternoon last November, he called me. His voice sounded gloomy, and he said he wanted me to come over. He wanted to talk about "us." I felt bad so I went over to his house. No one was home, even his dog was outside. He took me down to the basement to "show me a drawing" he had made. The basement was filled with tools and weight-lifting equipment. Off to the side was a little room with a bed.

I remember thinking, "Please, God, please, let us make up." He took me to where the bed was. He started kissing my neck gently. I loved it. I felt the way I used to feel when we first met— I felt loved. Then he started rubbing my breasts, and I let him do that because I still felt secure. It was so good being in his arms again. But, gradually, he started kissing me roughly, the kind of heavy kiss you'd expect from a crazed killer.

I told him no, to please stop, but he kept saying, "I love you. You know I won't hurt you. I missed you." Then he grabbed me by the arm, pulled me onto the bed, and started pressing roughly against my body. I tried to scream, but he had the radio on so loud I couldn't even hear myself breathe.

I was so scared. I was screaming, "Stop it! Get the f--k off me." All he said was "Shut up, shut up!" He started to unbutton my fly and I tried to push him off, pull his hair, bite his arm, and pinch him, but it was a lost cause. Then he pulled down my pants and started to push into me. I went into a state of freezing panic. I couldn't move or say anything. I was paralyzed.

When it was over he said, "You damn b--ch, can't even make me come, ah you're hopeless." He walked to another part of the room, and I made my move. I pulled my pants back on and I ran, ran as fast as I could.

That was the first time I had sex. It was horrible, and I felt I'd let him do it. I figured, "Well, I let him touch me and all so he had a right." Now I know it was his fault, not mine. I was raped.

I cried all night (except when my mom was looking). When I finally fell asleep, I had a horrible nightmare. In it, Maurice was on top of me again, but I managed to push him off. I grabbed one of his dumbbells, hit him in the head with it, and killed him. The dreams continue to this day. In some I actually like having sex with him.

Days passed and I didn't tell a soul because I still thought it was all my fault. Then my friend Jason came up to me while I was walking home from school and asked me, "Why'd you f--k Maurice?" He told me Maurice had started to spread rumors about how he f--ked me and all and I "sucked in bed."

I couldn't believe it. Even after everything he'd done, it was still amazing to me that he could be such a low-life. One time I walked past the local pizzeria and these girls I knew were standing by the corner. As I passed by they made comments like, "Oh, there goes the ho . . . she f--ked Maurice, she sucked his d--k, and she can't give a good f--k." I just gave them a dirty look and kept on walking.

Most of my friends believed the rumors too, and I started spending more and more time by myself. I even stopped communicating with my mom. We just grew apart—really it was me that grew away from her. She would constantly ask me what was wrong. "I'm just tired," I'd tell her. My mother is a smart woman and noticed that I was acting different. I looked down most of the time, and was starting to gain weight. Most importantly I had missed my period. She knew that because I get very crabby and bitchy around the time I get my period.

I knew I should have told her what happened, but I figured she'd say that I looked for it. I didn't want to hear that. I needed support, not an I-told-you-so.

Anyway, I just thought I looked down because I was tired, that I was gaining weight because I'd eaten too much, and missed my period because I was stressed out. My mom, on the other hand, asked me straight up: "¿*Estás embarazada?*" (Are you pregnant?)

"How dare you think such a thing?" I told her. "Just because I'm quiet and fat, that means I'm pregnant?" To me being pregnant was having a special glow and getting morning sickness (which I didn't get). Besides, I thought that in order to get pregnant the guy had to come inside of you, and that didn't happen to me. I was so stupid.

My mom told me she had a dream with me and a baby and lots

of blood. Dreams are very important to her. They are her way of predicting the future. After a while, I thought to myself, maybe I am pregnant. I felt my belly getting kind of hard, the way a pregnant woman's would. I thought about finding out for myself—just to make sure—but I wasn't sure where to go. My first thought was Planned Parenthood, but I was frantic. Where was it? How would I get there? I couldn't go alone—or could I?

And what if my mom found out? What would I do then? If I was pregnant, I didn't really want to know. So, all I did was go to church every Sunday and pray that I wasn't.

One cold December day my mom and I were on the train on our way to visit family when all of a sudden she told me that we were going to see a doctor. I didn't want to see a doctor, but there was no way out. At the doctor they did a urine test. I was scared, I mean really scared. What would I do if I were pregnant? What would my mother think? "My God, my God, why have you abandoned me?" I remember saying that to myself.

When I was called into the doctor's office, I noticed a little pink box with a plus sign in the middle. It looked just like one of those home pregnancy tests I'd seen on TV. But I didn't know whether it was mine or not. The doctor came in, looked toward the table where the thing was, and said she was sorry to inform me that I was pregnant. I looked at my mother and she looked at me. Tears of betrayal ran down her face, and tears of helplessness and anxiety came down mine. "It can't be!" I shouted, "Take another test!" I tried denying that I had had sex: "*¡Eso es imposible! He didn't even come!*"

The doctor told me a story about a girl who got pregnant just by being real close to the guy. I couldn't believe this was happening to me. My mother demanded that the doctor check to see if I was really still a virgin, like I was insisting. The doctor checked and said no, that I had lost my hymen (that's the thin lining in your vagina, your "cherry").

My mom looked at me with pain in her eyes and right away told the gynecologist, "*Sáquelo ahora mismo.*" (Take it out right now.) In other words, an abortion.

I couldn't say anything. I was in shock and I felt as if I no longer had control over my body. The nurse came over and stuck a needle in my right arm. "*No te preocupes*" (Don't worry), she said in a comforting, reassuring voice. Then I started to feel numb and was knocked out completely.

I don't remember anything after that. I never found out what kind of an abortion I had, or whether you could tell if it was male or female. All I remember was being dizzy afterward. I couldn't walk straight and was seeing double. I felt empty inside. I felt like I had committed some kind of crime. In a way I think I did.

I was also petrified of what was going to happen once we got home. My mom yelled and screamed. She told my aunts and they were shocked. They couldn't believe I would sleep with a guy at such a young age (14). I wanted to tell them the truth but I thought, "Where's the proof?" I knew Maurice would deny it, so I didn't bother.

For months I kept the truth inside. My mom would say things every now and then like "*Tú eres una puta . . . una desgraciada . . . tan inteligente y tan estúpida a la vez . . . una mal agradecida . . . un castigo de Dios.*" (You're a slut . . . a disgrace . . . so smart and so stupid at the same time . . . ingrate . . . this is God's punishment.) She would compare me to my cousin, and friends of the family who she considered well mannered and decent, a blessing to their families. What she didn't realize was that some of them were taking drugs and sleeping around.

Her cruelty and distrust in me drove us farther apart. I was forbidden to go out, wear makeup, use hairspray, buy new clothes, talk on the phone (unless it was about schoolwork), watch TV, or listen to the radio. I couldn't answer the phone—she assumed the caller was one of my lovers or something. I couldn't even go to school by myself, because she thought I would cut and meet my lovers. To this day, every morning, we take the same bus, and the same train. She told me that I won't be able to have a boyfriend till I'm in college. She won't let me go to my senior prom, no matter how well I do in school. And what hurt the most is she won't let me have the sweet 16 birthday party I always dreamed of. You know, with the guys in tuxedos, the girls in their gowns—me in my gown—with lots of flowers, and presents, dancing the waltz with my daddy, that kind of stuff. She said I didn't deserve it.

It started with Maurice. He took my virginity, he took my trust in others, he took me. I'll never be the same. After that, my mom stepped in and took my freedom. As for my so-called friends, I had to live with their rumors and insults. Every little thing I had was taken away from me.

So many things were happening to me at once. I was having bad dreams, failing math (I had never failed a subject in my life). I was fighting with my mom. I was fighting with my new boyfriend, Franco. I would fly into jealous rages, and he would complain that I wouldn't talk to him when I was upset or had something on my mind. I didn't know what to do; I wanted to kill myself.

I wrote a letter—more like a will—letting my mom know the truth, letting her know how much I loved her and how much I wanted her to be with my dad again (they have been divorced since I was about 4). I let my friends know why I had been so depressed and how I wanted them to remember me always. I left the letter in a book, in the school locker I shared with my good friend Annie. She found it, read it, and came up to me and asked me what had happened.

I was mad that she had invaded my privacy like that, but I felt the time had come for me tell someone. I had to. Annie was very supportive, but she kept suggesting that I tell my mother. I couldn't do that, I just couldn't.

I told a few other friends too—partly because I wanted them to learn not to always trust guys, but mainly because I needed to get some kind of communication going so I could feel better about myself. Everyone suggested I tell my mom the truth. I guess I will tell her someday. When, I'm not quite sure, but I will. Maybe when I get married or when I have a child. I don't want her to die without knowing the truth about the whole incident, and other incidents as well.

At times when I see a girl with a baby, I envy her. I watch TV and when shows come on about women giving birth, I envy them too. My baby would have been born in late August or mid-September of '91. Sometimes I try to imagine how my life would have changed if I had kept it. Would I still be in high school? Would my friends still be there for me the way they are now? Would I still be living with my mom? Would I still be going out with my boyfriend?

I wonder what my baby would have looked like. Would it have been a boy or a girl? I know I would still have loved the baby a lot, even though it wasn't conceived the way I would have wanted. My mom and I have talked about this a few times. She says it was good I had the abortion because otherwise, I would have gone through life not being able to do a lot of the things I wanted. It's funny because I feel trapped now—even without a child.

My mom tries to be the perfect mother, by asking me how my day was and stuff, but I just ignore her. I feel we can't communicate as well as we used to. If she's always going to doubt my word, why even bother trying?

I've had dreams about how I could have stopped the rape. Maybe I could have prevented it by hitting him harder, or by never going downstairs to the basement at all. But it's hard to think of that stuff at the time.

After I was raped, I started to read up about date rape, and I was surprised to learn that I wasn't the only one. I always used to hear about guys mugging and raping women in dark alleys, but I had never heard of this other, more common type of rape. I found out that even married women get raped by their husbands. (Yes, it can happen: married or not, when a woman says no she means NO. No ifs, ands, or buts about it!)

So many girls live through this terrible ordeal and don't tell anyone till years later—if at all. You rarely hear about it, unless it's on TV. Like the St. John's rape case. Even though she lost the case, I give the victim a lot of credit for having the guts to press charges. It was a very courageous thing to do. I feel more women should. Rape isn't our fault. I used to think I provoked it, but I don't anymore.

I still see Maurice around the neighborhood from time to time, and my bus passes by his house every day. I wish I didn't have to, but that's life. I don't look at him and he doesn't look at me. I've learned a lot during the year since it happened. I learned what real pain is like, and how hatred for someone you once loved can ruin you inside. At times when I seem cheerful, I'm suffering inside—all because of one guy, one day, and one nightmare.

If you have been raped the first thing you should do is go to a doctor and get yourself checked out. Don't put it off like I did. You never know what's going on inside your body. Then find someone you can trust, someone you feel safe with, like a sibling, a friend, or even a parent or relative, and tell them—talk to them. At times like that you need a lot of support. I recommend counseling too. I'll be getting counseling as soon as I think I'm ready. I know it'll help a great deal.

In the meantime, I have a wonderful boyfriend, Franco. It took me a long time to even consider trusting him, but I do. I've also come to realize that there are still a few decent people left in this world. No matter what, though, I always have to think three times before I start believing in them.

Epilogue

I originally wrote about my rape in *New Youth Connections (NYC)* to show other teens—especially girls—where relationships can sometimes lead.

I think another reason why I wrote the story was to reach one very special person—my mom. Even though I was afraid to tell her, deep down I wanted her to know, to understand what really happened.

When I first read the issue that had my story in it, I cried. My mom was there and I let her see me cry. She saw what I was reading and right away took out the copy I had given her and turned to that page. She read, and read, and read. Even though I had changed the names and some of the details, she recognized the story. Later that day, she asked me if I had written the article. I said no, but she kept asking until she finally got the truth out of me.

At first I felt much better—like a tremendous load was taken off me. Then when we talked about it, she made me feel cheap. "I told you never to go to his house when no one was home," she said. "You get what you look for."

That was exactly what I didn't need to hear. I was furious. How could she say that? I thought she would empathize, hold me, and say she was sorry it happened, but she didn't. She was really mad. Even madder that I didn't tell her sooner.

We let some time pass so both of us could cool off. Then one night she came into my room to talk about it. She told me how upset she was that I didn't tell her. "I am your mother," she kept saying. "I am the one person who you can trust. How could you tell all your friends and not me?"

It was hard for both of us. I was her one and only, and the thought of some punk hurting me hurt her even more. She said I was like a diamond—so precious and unique that you want to guard it and keep it safe at all times.

Things have gotten better since my mom and I talked. I'm still somewhat overprotected, but at least we're getting back that open and honest relationship we once had. I told her all about my newfound love, Franco, and our secret engagement. She wasn't so pleased about the engagement part—she said we were way too young for that. But she took it far better than I ever expected.

When I picked up the next issue of *NYC* and saw the letters to the editor about my story, I was so happy I started to cry again. One girl wrote, "It really made me think that my life is not a game. It's not all about cute guys but about how guys respect your feelings." And she is absolutely right, looks aren't everything. I remember thinking like that a year ago, but not anymore.

My editor showed me all the letters that didn't make it into the magazine. And I've even overheard people talking about the story in school (they didn't know I was the one who wrote it). I heard people say they really liked the writing and some even mentioned how they'll think twice before they get into that kind of situation. Somebody else said she realized how easy it is to get pregnant.

Other comments got me really pissed: "She should have told her moms—I would have," one girl said. Of course she can say that now. She isn't in the position I was and doesn't know how I felt, so she shouldn't have talked. Another one that bothered me was: "I felt sorry for her." I don't want anyone pitying me. I'd rather they just try to understand how I felt and learn something from my experiences. I still don't want people to know I am the girl who got raped. I want them to see me as the young lady who taught them a little lesson about life and trust.

I Never Thought
He'd Try to Kill Me

By Anonymous

I've published personal pieces before about the trials and turbulence of teenagehood, but I never thought I'd write a story with this title and hide behind an anonymous byline. And I certainly never expected the "he" would be Lewis, my boyfriend of thirteen months.

If anyone told me that Lewis would transform my eager anticipation of turning 18 and beginning college into a nightmare of brain damage and agony, I would have said, "You're crazy." That's what I said to my friends who met Lewis and told me to be careful because there was "something strange about him." They said he was too quiet, and seemed jealous of me. I resented and ignored these comments. Lots of people told me I was very mature and perceptive for my age and I liked to believe it. If there was something wrong with him, I'd definitely see it. So I asked those "Dear Abby" friends of mine to mind their own business. Fortunately, when these same people came to visit me in the hospital, not one of them said aloud the I-told-you-sos that seemed to fill their eyes.

Our fight took place on a deceptively beautiful day in early May. We got into an argument in part over sex and in part over nonsense. Before I knew what was happening, Lewis threw me on the couch and hovered over me with a baseball bat. All I could do was plead "Stop! Stop!" as the heavy wood smashed my skull. I couldn't believe he was doing this since he never came close to hitting me before.

The image of him standing over me with a cold stare as I lay on the floor with blood rushing out of my head, and my hands raised to get him to help me, will forever be tattooed on my memory. When I awoke in the hospital four days later, doctors stood over me trying to see if I was as brain damaged as they had predicted. I couldn't talk, but I managed to write, "Am I okay?"

My comatose daze didn't spare me further humiliation. Every serious head injury patient has to go through a battery of psychiatric tests to determine if the injury caused certain problems. I can't capture in words how I felt when the hospital psychiatrist asked me if I actually "enjoyed" the beating. Or when two friends walked into my room as mashed potatoes slid out of my mouth because I could barely swallow.

But nothing could match the police visits, which left me feeling like a criminal. Only hours after I came out of the coma, the police made me describe (in writing since I was temporarily mute) the extent of our sexual relationship in near graphic detail, since our argument was caused in part by sex. I just wanted to go home. There I was at the doorstep of my 18th birthday and people were treating me like a physical and emotional invalid.

I came home to discover that the police suspected Lewis was a drug user because of "strange" messages he left on my answering machine. We had a lot of stupid private jokes that might seem "druggish" to the serious listener. But why should I have to explain that to anyone? And how did they find out, anyway? I soon discovered that, thanks to the police and gossip, almost everyone knew that my boyfriend used my head for batting practice. To this day, that's the first thing some people bring up when they see me. Ms. Goody Two-Shoes became Ms. Jennifer Levin [the young woman who was strangled to death by Robert Chambers while they were having sex in Central Park].

My speech was seriously impaired. To escape, I became obsessed with my therapy exercises and tried every trick in the book to get my paralyzed tongue to move. But I just couldn't escape the concerned and the nosy who wanted to know more. I kept on hearing how good I looked—"considering." I think a few people were slightly disappointed that my head wasn't bandaged or shaved and my hair did a pretty good job of covering the scars. People wanted to know if I was going to press full charges or even drop them in exchange for intense psychiatric care for Lewis and a court order that he forever stay far away from me. I never got the chance to decide.

On June 1, a detective called to tell me that they found Lewis—but he was dead. They found him floating off a pier a mile away from his house in Brooklyn. I was given the false impression that he killed himself out of remorse. That did more damage to me than the baseball bat. But I'll get to that later.

For a while it appeared the attack would only bring a minor hearing loss and temporarily impaired speech. But in late June, I took the English Regents and bombed on it. The little writing I did was forced and poor by my standards. And ever since I came out of the coma, thinking clearly was a struggle. In July I went to a neuropsychologist who put me through grueling but extensive testing. She determined the blows to the head caused a language agnosia (a serious language impairment) and some cognitive dysfunction (a blockage of thought processes). I was also suffering from a case of something called receptive aphasia (a lesion in the brain that causes a communication problem). She referred me to another neuropsychologist and began hinting that I start thinking of other careers besides journalism and professional writing.

Since the fifth grade, becoming a writer had been an obsessive dream and now a doctor was telling me I may never be able to realize that dream. Even if I could express the kind of devastation I felt, I wouldn't—it's just too painful. It was the kind of pain I'm battling right now as I sit at this computer trying to say things, but settling for inferior ways of saying them. In September I started college, against the neuropsychologist's advice, in the hope of proving her wrong. I put up a fierce struggle to wade through my studies while putting on a phony smile and personality to get by socially. I even made some new friends.

But emotionally I was breaking down and guilt made it difficult to keep the feelings in check. All I could think of was that Lewis would still be alive if I had given in to the sexual stuff. I kept thinking of how a detective had told me that Lewis's aunt said "he punished himself" in commenting on his suicide. I refused to do the exercises the neuropsychologist said were crucial if I wanted to start thinking better. I didn't think I had a right to get better. To punish myself, I quit a part-time job I loved. I even went out to Lewis's grave a few times to say, "I'm sorry."

My father was getting pretty worried. In October, he called the private investigator who had been searching for Lewis almost from the start and asked him to tell me everything he knew. In my three-hour visit to his office, I learned more about Lewis's past than I knew about my own. Two weeks after Lewis was buried, the P.I. had phone conversations with Lewis's mother and uncle under false pretexts. He also read the police psychology report on Lewis's suicide and the medical examiner's report.

First of all, Lewis didn't kill himself the night he attacked me. Someone in his family was hiding him for weeks and, for a complicated reason, it's even possible most of his family didn't know about it. The most incredible piece of evidence the P.I. had was that Lewis went bowling while I was in the hospital with black eyes! This was all backed up by the medical report, which estimated he was dead for only around four days when he was found, four weeks after the attack. And it seems that he didn't kill himself only because of what he did to me. The police psychology report listed him as suicidal for a long time. His mental health had been withering away since his father's death in '85 and he had a lot of problems I never knew about. He got into a vicious verbal fight with his mother two days before he beat me, for example. He probably did to me what he wanted to do to her. I could go on and on.

"Then why," I asked the P.I., "couldn't someone—anyone— from his family say, 'He was very unstable for a long time and had a lot of emotional problems you didn't know about. The details are private and it's too difficult to speak to you. Please understand. Good-bye'?" After all, I was given the impression that he was fine until he attacked me. Those words or something similar would have made a world of difference and speeded my recovery.

The P.I. just shook his head and got really annoyed. "When are you going to realize that to Lewis's family you were nothing more than a piece of ass he spent his weekends with? They wouldn't have given a damn if he killed you. They don't remember your name and probably think Lewis smashed your skull in self-defense."

A piece of ass he spent his weekends with. Even though the P.I.'s words were very harsh, they were probably very true. His aunt was nastier than the flu as she denied me permission to attend Lewis's funeral. And his older sister refused to speak to me when I called to express my condolences since she was one of the few relatives Lewis ever claimed to care about. No one ever expressed any remorse for what their flesh and blood did to his girlfriend and no one was willing to talk to me for three minutes, like I very much wanted. And of course, no one had the morality to call just once to see if I even was recovering. I was stupid enough to take that to mean I was being blamed for what happened. But they were just cold and low-class people who didn't give a damn.

Suddenly, my anchor of guilt dropped and a victim's anger set in. I didn't deserve to be smashed in the head and I didn't deserve to feel guilty. I was a victim and I received no justice. I needed to feel that anger so it could be transformed into a determination to get better. I'm determined to prove the neuropsychologist wrong and overcome those brain defects the way I overcame my speech impediment. I'm speaking normally now and I believe I'll regain the writing and thinking abilities I'm supposed to have lost and will become a stronger person for it. I won't let the sickness of one person destroy my future. You shouldn't either, if you've been the victim of a vicious crime.

Believe it or not, I'm still sorry that Lewis is dead even though a bulldozer couldn't drag me to his grave again. He never would have beat me if he had gotten help for his problems and he'd still be alive if he had turned himself in after the attack. It's really a shame—he had a lot going for him and he had just turned 21.

I've lost a lot of self-respect. I was used and I don't think Lewis was capable of loving me or anyone else. I realize I wasn't the very mature and perceptive person people said I was. I was just some naive teen whose poor judgment nearly cost her her life. Even though they were vague, Lewis gave me signals and warnings that I just ignored. I don't know when or if I'll ever be able to trust my judgment again.

What happened to me had a one in a million chance of happening. And that guy you're dating right now is probably just as wonderful as you think he is. But keep your ears open and listen, *really listen* to what other people have to say. And pay attention to cues and warnings that show unstable behavior. If I had, I wouldn't have spent my graduation day in a neurologist's office. Remember, you'll probably never go through something like this. But pay attention. One in a million is one too many.

The Anger Can Go Somewhere Else

By Anonymous

It happened on the night that I met up with some friends at a party in the Bronx. I'd been mad at my girl all day—she had dissed me by playing me out in my own neighborhood, dumping me for another guy who had more money. I was livin' small and the other boy, a drug dealer, was livin' large and trying to play hard. We had a stare at each other, the drug dealer and me. So I figured I'd forget about the gold-digger, but I was still mad on my way to the party.

There were twenty boys at the party and only three girls. (Not very good-looking girls, either.) We were bored and there was not a damn thing to do. So at 2:00 in the morning we went outside and started throwing bottles at each other and at other people in the park. Then we saw some guy walking by himself. At first we thought he had a gun because he was a young guy and it was late at night. But then he started walking fast, so we surrounded him. He got scared and begged us not to hurt him.

He gave up his watch and a few other things. Then he walked away.

I had a hammer in my hand, because this was the first time I'd been to a party in the Bronx and I never leave home without something (except when I'm going to school—I don't need it there). One of my friends, Allen, snatched the hammer from me, hit the guy in the back, and the guy swung on him, so we had to rush him and f--k his sh-t up. I was already mad and this added more pressure to the pile.

We all kicked and punched him, hit him with bottles and the hammer. I kicked and punched him in the face until he was down on the ground. It felt good—I felt this adrenaline rush, like I was unstoppable. Then we jetted and we bragged about it all the way home. "Yo," we kept saying, "did you see the way I f--ked his sh-t up?" We all laughed about what each of us did. There was blood all over Allen's jacket.

Afterward there were times when I felt sorry for the guy, that he had to be put in that position. What happened that night had a lot to do with the male ego—the need to be a show-off, as well as the need to take out our anger on someone. I was mad at everybody because my girl had dumped me, and my only friends were people who didn't talk much if something was bothering them—they solved everything with their fists.

Now I see that this anger can go somewhere else, either by talking it out or by getting something like a punching bag. When I get mad now, I usually start working out and it helps. I'm not so eager to follow what the group does. I realize how wrong I was that night and that there's a better way.

I never did it again. And so far it's gonna stay that way, unless someone steps to me. No more games after that. Because nowadays it's kill or be killed, and I ain't havin' it.

Cops and Kids

Reaction to the Anthony Baez Verdict

Getting Away with Murder

Dear *New Youth Connections,*

The criminal justice system is no good because it tells cops they can do anything they want. Look at the Baez-Livoti case. When Officer Livoti confronted Baez because of a football hitting the window of his cop car, he put an illegal choke hold on Baez. He didn't know Baez had asthma, which may have been a part of what caused Baez to die. In the court trial, Livoti was found not guilty of criminally negligent homicide because the judge said the prosecution hadn't proven that it was the choke hold alone that killed him. But if it wasn't for the choke hold, Baez would still be here.

This is just one example of what cops are allowed to do and get away with. Until there is someone in office who realizes what is going on in the criminal justice system, the system will not change. We need somebody to take charge and control the police so that they don't commit these injustices.

Chris Cabezas

Something's Wrong

Dear *New Youth Connections,*
Police officer Francis X. Livoti deserves to be given the death penalty. He choked Anthony Baez to death and they still found him not guilty. I really don't know why Livoti wasn't found guilty. What he did was very wrong. Something is really wrong here, and we need to do something fast, before it's too late.

Janice Roman

Punched in the Ribs

Dear *New Youth Connections,*
Two years ago at the 18th Avenue Feast, a friend of mine was drinking a beer and watching the crowd go by. An officer walked over and told him to dump the beer. So he did with no problems.

As my friend walked away in silence the officer asked him, "Are you a wise guy?" "No," he replied. Then the officer smacked him in the back of his head.

I got punched in the ribs once because while I was speaking to a cop, I pointed at something. He hit me and said, "Don't raise your hand." I was only 12 then but I guess the age and size of little me didn't faze him. I never forgot that hit.

Cops should be watched at all times. They walk the streets with an imaginary crown on their heads. Cops should be more educated and not too young. I'm not saying cops are stupid but when you have more education you have several ways to handle problems. They should be at least 25 years old, and have a college diploma and two years of police training. The smarter the cops, the safer the streets.

Frank Lamberti

Cops and O.J. Get Off

Dear *New Youth Connections,*

　The so-called "law enforcers" break the law themselves. The badge gets to their head and they think they can push people around and get away with it.

　The sad thing is most of the time they do. They treat people horribly and are not around when you need them.

　Our court system is also in a shambles. Two kinds of people have the advantage. They are the celebrities and the police officers. When you have money you can pay for bail, get better lawyers, and have a much better chance of getting off. Take the O. J. Simpson trial. He got so much media attention and had so much money to pay for those expensive lawyers that he got off. It was amazing that all the evidence against him meant nothing.

　I think everyone should be equal no matter what their occupation or wealth.

Nichole Guglielmo

Cops and Kids

Reported by Julio A. Garcia

About a year ago, Eric Smith, 19, of the High School for the Liberal Arts, was on a class trip when he was stopped by two cops. "They tried to make me take all my stuff out of my bag, just so that they could check it out," he said. Eric tried to find out why they were harassing him, but they just kept telling him to empty his bag. Then his teacher came up and explained that they were on a school trip and the class continued on. "They just go around telling us what to do," said Eric, who to this day remembers the embarrassment he felt in that situation.

Eric isn't the only teenager who feels disrespected or threatened by the police. "They come round here thinkin' they're the man, and try to tell me where to go and what to do," said Roberto, 18, who I found hanging out in front of my building. To Roberto, they're just "a bunch of fat n--gas, looking to kick some ass."

Teenagers I spoke to around the city said they were wary of

the police and complained that they or people close to them had
had bad, sometimes brutal experiences. Alex Stephen, 16, of
Brooklyn Tech High School, said her cousin was beaten up by
cops in 1989. Pedro Nieves, 19, said he and his friend were
stopped by police and when his friend couldn't show them identification they arrested him because they claimed he looked like a
suspect in a robbery.

Incidents like these make many young people mistrustful,
even afraid of cops. Though her worst experiences with the police have been when they've told her and her friends to move
along, Jessica Jenkins, 20, of City College, says there are times
when a person can't help but look at a cop and get scared. "Like
if you was in an alley, and going somewhere, when you see a cop
car, you can feel something jump inside of you," she explained.

"Historically, it's been an adversarial relationship," said Lieu-
tenant Arthur Doyle, who recently retired as commanding officer of the Police Department's Youth Services Division. One of
the reasons for this, he feels, is that the police are the ones people
call to report disorderly conduct: "Get off the corner," "Turn
that music down," "Where's your bus pass?" and things like that.
And, according to Doyle, teens "don't always see what they're
doing as disorderly" so they end up feeling picked on.

When it comes to police suspicion toward teens, Doyle says it
comes about "the same way all prejudices are formed." Much of
the crime that's committed in this city, he explained, is committed by young people, and unfortunately, when officers "see the
same people" repeatedly breaking the law, "you form an opinion
that all teenagers are up to something." But he stressed that
"that's not an opinion that's shared by all officers."

While all cops may not be prejudiced against us, "too many
police officers view all teens as possible criminals," said Richie
Pérez of the National Congress for Puerto Rican Rights, an organization that works to protect and defend the rights of the
Puerto Rican people and other minority groups. "They don't respect the rights of young people." Pérez says the police regularly
violate young people's rights through illegal searches and arbi-

trary commands, like "I don't want you waiting at this train station, take the next train and get out of here."

One reason for this kind of misconduct is the young age of many officers. In spite of their training, Doyle says that "people that age often don't have the life experience" to be able to handle the situations they face on the street.

But regardless of how old they are or how many years they've been on the force, Pérez says that "some officers don't live in the city and know nothing of the communities [they patrol]." He thinks they often have racist attitudes toward those communities and are taught in the police academy that "it's us against the world." All of this makes them view the communities and teenagers they are supposed to be serving as the enemy.

Doyle agrees that many of these problems exist, but feels it's not something unique to the police. "If you were brought up to disrespect people," he said, "you're going to disrespect [them] no matter what profession you go into." As for the infamous "blue wall of silence," where cops look the other way while other cops break the rules or unofficially punish the ones who speak up about it, Doyle says that's something that "exists in almost any profession."

But Pérez says that police work isn't just any profession. "They have one of the most difficult jobs in society," he explained. Because we allow them to carry guns and make life-and-death decisions, Pérez feels society has a responsibility to monitor their activities closely and punish them severely when they abuse their authority. When we fail in that responsibility, it can often have consequences far beyond people getting their feelings hurt. According to Pérez, after the Puerto Rican Day parade in June, one Bushwick teenager was allegedly punched in the face by a cop, and another Maced while already in handcuffs.

Last January, New York City detectives shot robbery suspects Anthony Rosario, 18, and 21-year-old-Hilton Vega twenty-two times. Medical experts say they appear to have been shot while lying face down on the floor and the case is still under investigation.

Pérez feels that as long as cops don't get punished even for the most severe forms of misconduct, their attitudes are not likely to change. He also believes there should be a law that requires police officers to live within the city limits and that they should receive better education about the cultures of the communities they serve.

Doyle agrees that police officers who break the law should be treated like any other lawbreaker. But he's not enthusiastic about the value of special training designed to make police more sensitive to the feelings of people in the community. "Coursework and street work are different," he said.

For him, the solution lies in recruitment of more minority officers. "People from some backgrounds have a certain understanding which can take the tension out of the situation," he said. Doyle, who is Black and grew up in the South Bronx, gave the example of seeing young Black males "acting macho." "I can identify with that," he said, explaining that he feels he is often in a better position to judge when a Black teenager's rowdy behavior and tough talk is just that and when it is something potentially dangerous or criminal. As for the use of force, Doyle said that an officer who's comfortable in the community is less likely to feel threatened or overreact to a teenager's behavior.

Like Pérez, my neighbor Roberto feels that mayor ought to "put a tight leash on [police] and make sure [they behave]." But none of the people I spoke to were terribly optimistic about that happening or relations improving anytime soon. "Not under a city administration that feels cops can do no wrong," said Pérez. "And not during times when poor communities are under attack," he added, referring to severe budget cuts in education, health care, and social programs, which he feels demonstrate the government's outright hostility toward poor people.

"It ain't never gonna change, so what's the point in askin'?" said Jessica Jenkins. "[Not] as long as they got the power." Her solution is "always try to avoid [police] as much as possible."

But for Doyle the best hope is for young people to join the police force and make a difference from within. "How are you going to change things," he asked, "if you don't become a part of them?"

Caught in the Act

By Rance Scully

One night a couple of summers ago, three of my friends and I were walking home from a party in Flatbush. It was around midnight and there was nobody around and no cars passing by. Then we realized that a patrol car was following about fifty feet behind us.

We knew we weren't talking loud enough to be disturbing anyone or doing anything else wrong, so we tried not to pay too much attention. But when I glanced over my shoulder the car was still there and getting even closer.

"Come on guys, let's get out of here," said one of my friends.

"Are you crazy?" I replied. "If we run, they'll definitely think we did something wrong."

It was obvious that they were watching us so I came out with another idea: "Why don't we go up to them and try and make conversation?" I said.

"What?" said one of my friends. "You must be out of your mind."

"What's wrong with that?" I said. "I'll do all the talking. I'll tell them where we're coming from and that we're on our way home." I was newly arrived from Jamaica and still had a lot to learn about life in New York.

My friends reluctantly agreed, and I turned around and headed in the direction of the patrol car. Suddenly, a blinding light shined on us and a voice on a loudspeaker ordered us to put our hands in the air and spread our legs.

Three cops got out of the car with guns drawn and pointed at us. I was scared and did what I was told.

"What do you guys think you're doing?" said one of them in a loud and aggressive tone.

I started to say something, but he told me to shut up and speak when I was spoken to. They placed their guns back into their holsters and searched us thoroughly. Then they ordered us to put our hands back down.

"Tell me where some of the players are around here and we won't arrest you," said another one.

"Excuse me, Officer," I said. "I don't know what you're talking about."

The three of them talked amongst themselves for a long time and then got into their car and sped off without another word.

That was my first encounter with the New York City Police Department, and trust me, I was so pissed off that I promised myself I would have nothing to do with them ever again.

Rikers:
Frontin' for Respect

By José R.

What's up, man? You wasn't getting up 7:30 in the morning in New York. But if I don't get up now the C.O. will be by my cell in about five minutes and then I'll have to answer to him. Man, if he ain't have that badge on his chest he won't be sh-t. If I was in New York . . .

Damn the world, damn this place and everyone in it. Got to brush my teeth, wash my face, and comb my hair. Got my fly clothes on. Got to show brothers I'm living large. Yup, got the fly kicks on too. I'm looking proper.

Time to walk out for school. Hold up, let me just flex in the mirror right quick and make sure everything is in the right burner. Can't go nowhere without my burner. Just in case a brother try and front. All right, got some brothers checking me out. How do they do it?

Oh yeah, just keep your arms pretty much still. Don't swing

'em, just move your shoulders and bop to the side a little. Yeah, now you got the walk, let's work on the face I'm gonna wear for the rest of the day. Okay, keep your jaws tight, squint your eyes a little. Now, drop your eyebrows. That's it. I'm on a roll now. Man, am I a trooper or what? Yeah, that'll put fear in their heart. They won't even look at me no more. They better not.

Man, I hate walking in damn line, like we're in grade school or something. We're passing another house. Look hard. You ain't new to this. A little more on the walk ... right, riiight. What's that? Mod 11? Man, them brothers are ass! Get ready, if any jump off, just keep swinging. Keep on looking hard. Yeah, they know better. Our house is the chop shop. I really could do without the riot squad though.

The riot squad. Man, listen ... if I was in New York ...

Man, these teachers be buggin' out. What I need to know all this geometry stuff for? As long as I can count my money, I'm straight. Man, what I need to come to school for anyway? I wasn't going to school in New York. Well, I was, but it sure wasn't for no geometry—them girls was fly. These teachers be looking good, too. Man, if I was in New York ...

Good, it's time to go back and eat chow. That's just the word to describe it. Chow. Chow-chow is more like it. They must be buggin' if they think I'm gonna eat this. Besides, that lady C.O. over there looks kind of good. If she sees me eating this it'll cramp my style.

Man, I shot fifty bags every week in commissary. Moms be looking out. Yeah, I know things are kind of rough at home, but I'm her son. She can't dis me like that. Yo, the C.O. looked at me. Yeah, you know I look good. I'll take her out for some steak any day, cause man if I was in New York ...

Man, I hate locking in for this count. Four-thirty, time to lock out. Right on time. Oh yeah, I'm gonna watch cartoons today, and if those brothers change the channel we'll just have to get it on. Yeah, you better not change that channel, cause when I was in New York ...

What's that new jack with the fly kicks on? He's gonna have to hop out of them. Let me send my little man to get them, cause if I got to take this razor out my ass, man, listen . . .

Look at him—he's scared to death. Yeah, that's it, give up them sneakers. Man, that jacket looks kind of fly too. Naw, I'll leave him with that at least. Herb. But if we was in New York . . .

What time is it? Yup, it's about that time for me to get up on the phone. Yeah, you see me coming, get up off the phone. What? Oh, calm down baby, he only asked for one more minute. Man, I was ready to blow something. I'll give him that minute, but if we was in New York . . .

"Hi, Ma. Yeah, I'm okay, how are you? Good. Well, Ma, I just called to see how you were doing. Are you coming up to see me tomorrow? Ma, put some money in my commissary. About fifty dollars, all right? Yeah, Ma, I know you need to pay the bills, but I need money too. Okay, then the sneakers, right? No, I don't want Reeboks. I wanted Nikes. Forget it! Just bring the sneakers. Ma, I gotta go, okay? Love you. Bye."

Why do these guys have to be all in my face when I'm on the phone? At least they know I get what I want. Cause when I was in New York . . .

Man, this day went by crazy fast. We had some dog food for dinner today again. Man, I couldn't even eat it and I was type hungry. If that guy didn't get cut in the mess hall, maybe I could've at least gotten a chance to eat my rice. That dude cut him up bad, too. At least thirty stitches right next to his eye. Not but four yards away from me either. I seen it coming, too. Thought he was coming for me. Would have cut him right back though, cause when I was in New York . . .

Man, I hate watching the cell door close every night. Be locked in like some animal. I ain't no animal.

"Yo! Y'all stop yelling out your cells. I'm trying to go to sleep." Bunch of cell gangsters. It's kind of a relief though to have this door closed behind me. At least now I know I'm safe. Ain't no razor cutting through that.

Almost forgot to pray. Lord, thanks for keeping me safe. I

could have been the one who got cut, and man was I scared. I could feel myself shaking while we were on the wall. I'm glad no one else saw me though. I thought they were gonna pick me for a herb. But they didn't. Thanks for that too. I know I did wrong when I took that guy's sneakers, but they were all looking at me when I came in the day room. You know, all my friends waiting to see what I would do. I'm really sorry though. I gave him another pair and they weren't that bad.

Lord, I hate having to act like a gangster, but if I don't then I'll be nowhere with no respect. But Lord, why do I feel that even if I'm acting this way, I get no respect?

Lord, my mother seemed pretty upset today. I really hurt her. I wanted to tell her how much I love her and not to worry, but my mans was around me. I know they were listening to my conversation, I had to keep strong cause I know she would have made me start crying and that would have been it.

Oh Lord, I'm so scared. I'm so lonely. I don't know what to do. I want to go home. Please, God, if you let me go home, I'll stop selling drugs and stuff. I'll stop acting like a gangster. God, please. Amen. Good night.

What's up, man? You wasn't getting up 7:30 in New York . . .

At the time this story was written, José R. was a student at the Rikers Island Educational Facility. The story was originally published in Streams 6, *a yearly anthology of student writing published by the Waterways Project, 393 St. Pauls Avenue, Staten Island, NY 10304.*

Busted

By Ligeia Minetta

The names of teens in this story have been changed.

The East Village on a Saturday night is a haven for almost every type of person imaginable, from wandering junkies on a quest for their next hit to tourists shopping for T-shirts and little Statues of Liberty. And it isn't uncommon for my friends and me to hang out there, going to concerts or just sitting for hours in one of the local coffee shops gabbing about nothing in particular. So the fact that a bunch of us were sitting on a stoop next to Munchy's Deli on St. Mark's Place on the night of November 26, 1996, at around 9:20 p.m. was nothing unusual.

It wasn't unusual that a patrol car pulled up, either, or that two chubby cops got out of the car and started walking toward us. You see, technically you're not allowed to hang out on a stoop unless you live there, and if the cops see more than a couple of people doing it they'll tell you to move along.

Figuring this was just business as usual, a couple of us got up and stood out on the sidewalk trying to decide what to do next.

My friend Jane had to go to the bathroom so we went off in search of a place that would let us use their potty.

When we got back onto the street there was still a large group of people at the corner (most of whom we knew because we had all just come from a concert about fifteen blocks away). As Jane and I walked back toward them, we noticed that the patrol car had not left yet either—which was odd, because we'd been gone at least ten minutes. Then we saw another car and a police van and hurried to see what was going on.

A couple of officers from the second patrol car had one guy backed up against the metal gate of a brownstone on the other side of the street and were talking to him about something. We figured they probably caught him with an open bottle of beer or something stupid, but I crossed over anyway, because I felt like being nosy.

I asked a couple of people if they knew what was going on, but before I could get an answer I heard screaming and yelling from behind me. I turned around to see two more officers grab my friend Danny. They got a hold of him, grabbed his arm, twisted it behind his back, and threw him down face first. When they pulled him up, blood was streaming down his chin and onto his leather jacket and army pants.

At the time, Danny and I were very close friends, and I flipped. I darted across the busy street (probably in front of a car, I didn't even notice) and started screaming, "Let him go! He didn't do anything!" Of course I didn't know if he'd done anything or not. I mean, for all I knew, they were picking him up on murder charges. But I didn't care, Danny was like my brother, and the cops were hurting him.

The cops cuffed Danny and put him in the back of the police van. But even though they told us to leave, no one did. And I wasn't the only one yelling. There must have been fifty of us. A tall White officer with a brown mustache held his club over his head as if to say, "If you come any closer I'll hit you," to the crowd. Then a female officer with chin-length dirty blond hair told me to back up. When I didn't move, she shoved me. I took a few steps backward and after I caught myself, I yelled, "Don't touch me, b--ch!"

That's when someone grabbed my arm, twisted it behind me the same way they had Danny's, and threw me up against the police van. While I was pinned against it, I felt something hard hit me on the back of my head. I didn't see stars or anything—I didn't even get a bump—it just hurt for a while when I touched it.

An officer, whose name I later learned was Cunningham, put handcuffs on me. Then he led me around to the other side of the van, where the door was. I climbed in, which wasn't as easy as it sounds—the van was at least two feet off the ground, and I'm only five foot four, plus my hands were cuffed behind my back. Cunningham slammed the door behind me and I walked to the back and sat down next to Danny.

After a few minutes, I heard my name being called from outside of the van. I couldn't see too well out the dirty back windows, but finally I spotted my friend Chip waving his arms. When he saw that he'd gotten my attention, he told me he would call my mom and tell her what happened. "Okay," I said loudly, and nodded my head up and down just in case he couldn't hear me.

Next into the van was my then boyfriend, Andrew, who took a seat in front of Danny and me and didn't seem upset about the situation at all. Then they threw Dave, a kid from Bergen County, New Jersey, into the van. His head, adorned with a brown spiked Mohawk, landed at my feet. He was crying in pain and couldn't see because he had been Maced (after he had been handcuffed, he told me).

Dave lay there on his stomach with his hands cuffed behind his back on the way to the 9th Precinct. When we got there, they opened the sliding door and because of the way Dave was wedged up against the door, he just kind of rolled out of the van and into the middle of 5th Street. As he lay there the officers taunted him, saying things like, "You cry like a b--ch."

An officer named Kohlar led me inside, through the lobby, and stopped at a doorway where there was a dirty old cardboard sign that said in orange letters No Firearms Past This Point. He gave in his gun, walked me through a big room with a lot of cops sitting at desks, up some stairs, and along a corridor lined with small holding cells to the very last one. An officer sitting outside it unlocked the large iron door to the cell and I stepped inside. No one who arrested me had bothered to read me my rights, never mind tell me what I was being charged with.

My friends Helen and Cathy were already in there. Helen had a large bump on her head from being whacked in the head twice—once with a walkie-talkie and once with a billy club. The second blow knocked her unconscious for a few moments, she said. When she came to, she was in handcuffs and her eyes were stinging with Mace. The Mace still had not worn off and Helen was crying. There was a sink in the cell where she could have washed her eyes out, but we were all still in handcuffs.

I sat down on a green bed-type thing next to her, and Cathy sat across from us on a metal bench. Fifteen or twenty minutes later, a female officer came and took us downstairs, one by one, to be searched. On the way, a young male cop with blond hair asked us to give some basic information, like our names, ages, and addresses.

I was the last one to be removed from the cell to be searched. As a short Hispanic lady led me back down the steep metal staircase, I was worried that I would lose my balance, confused because I didn't know what was happening, and just plain tense. She took me to a room with bare cinder block walls and chalky dust on the floor. Then she uncuffed me and instructed me to take off my jacket and my boots.

I unlaced my boots as quickly as possible and stood up. She told me to lean up against the back wall and spread 'em. She gave me the basic pat down/frisk type deal that you get on the way into some clubs and concerts. Then she took my jewelry and some other stuff from my jacket pocket and put it in a little bag. She counted my money and gave it back to me and then filled out some papers that Cunningham, the arresting officer, later had to sign. Unfortunately, they never gave me a property slip so I could retrieve my belongings after I was released. That was the last time I saw any of my stuff, including my house keys and my favorite necklace.

After that they put the cuffs back on me and led me back upstairs to the holding cell. About five minutes later, Helen, Cathy, and I were all taken back downstairs to the main office and put on a bench next to the cell where Danny and Dave were. Danny's face looked a little better, but now Dave's face was bleeding because, according to him, the officer who led him into the station had smashed his face into the corner of a soda machine.

Andrew and another guy, named Joey, were cuffed to the outside corner of the cell. They were both 15 and therefore considered juveniles so the cops couldn't put them inside. (Anyone 16 or over is an adult in the eyes of the New York State criminal justice system.) My right hand was also cuffed to the cell, Cathy was cuffed to my left hand, and Helen was cuffed to a StairMaster! Soon the cops took Andrew and Joey into another room and cuffed them to a heating pipe. At around 1 a.m. their parents came and they were both released.

The five of us who were 16 and over sat in the station for hours doing nothing. While we were there they brought different people in and out of the boys' cell. First off there was a man named Miguel who was there for hopping a turnstile. Then there was a cute guy we dubbed Drug Dealer Boy who was arrested for selling crack and then trying to bribe his arresting officer.

PsychoLoco was an extremely gorgeous guy who had been arrested for fighting. He definitely earned the name we gave him. When he first got there, and the cops put him in the cell with the other guys, he sat alone in the corner holding something like a tissue on his bloody right hand and just sort of growled at the other males. Every time one of them opened their mouths to say anything at all, he would growl out, between clenched teeth, "Shut the f--k up!" And they did!

During our time at the precinct we were each allowed our one phone call. I called my mother, who had already heard what had happened from Chip, and had been calling the precinct to find out what was going on. I thought she'd be angry but she took it really well. She said the police had told her there was nothing she could do, that even if she came down, they wouldn't let her see me. They said I was going to be charged with two felonies—riot in the first degree and assault—and they were going to put me and my friends through the system.

There was nothing Helen, Cathy, and I could do to pass the time except talk about our situation, the cops, and the two cute boys inside the cell. Then we started talking about how pathetic we were that we'd just been arrested, and we were still checking out guys! Occasionally a song we knew would come on the radio and we would sing along.

One by one, they took us to have our fingerprints taken on this big electronic scanner that was supposed to speed up the process of checking our criminal records by transmitting the prints directly to Albany. But the 9th Precinct ended up losing all of our prints and they had to be retaken the old-fashioned way—with ink—about twenty-four hours later when we were downtown at Central Booking. (Even when this doesn't happen, a person's first arrest can often take the longest, because the computer in Albany has to look through all the records to see if it can find a set of matching prints.)

We were seated in a big room with a lot of desks. About eight or ten cops, both in and out of uniform, were sitting around doing paperwork and talking about a test they had just taken.

After a while they decided to pick on us. The first insult came from a short, balding, White man with a light brown mustache and wire-rimmed glasses. He told Cathy, whose blond hair was shaved nearly bald, except for a tuft of fluffy bangs in the front, and who had thick black circles painted around her eyes, that he wouldn't like to wake up next to her in the morning.

We knew it was pointless to talk back, that it would only make our time there even more unbearable. Instead I just rolled my eyes at the ugly cop's comment about my friend, slumped back against the wall, and rested my right boot on the lower bar of the holding cell. A tall White police officer with short, dark brown hair and a thinnish mustache noticed the way I was sitting. "Look," he remarked to his fellow officers with a smile, "she's trained, she opens right up for me."

I wanted to get up and brutally murder that man, but I knew that's exactly the reaction he wanted, so I just made a face that kind of said, "Whatever." He went on to say that the three of us, meaning the female contingent, needed Lysol between our legs, and referred to us as h-s. I was praying that my lovely visit to the 9th Precinct would come to an end. And soon my prayers were answered.

Finally, at about 4 a.m., they cuffed our hands behind our backs again and told us we were being taken downtown to Central Booking. We were all escorted back into a police van and driven down to Centre Street in lower Manhattan.

The process of checking into Central is simple and fairly quick. In fact, it doesn't really involve anyone but the officers who brought you there. You and the police wait on a line until you get to the guards sitting at a counter, where they hand over your paperwork and then take you upstairs to see the nurse. (At this point the sexes are separated again, but this time for good.)

Cathy, Helen, and I lined up in the hallway outside of the door to the nurse's office and were called in one at a time. When it was my turn, the nurse asked me basic female health questions, like whether I was pregnant and/or needed to go to the hospital.

I asked the nurse if I could have a cup of water from the sink. I was dying of thirst, and when I had asked for water at the 9th they basically laughed in my face. She said yes, however, and soon Helen joined me in drinking as much water as we could manage before they took us to the place where they hold women captive until they get arraigned.

At this point I had to get strip-searched. But after the night I'd just had, one more type of humiliation was the least of my problems. I took off all my clothes. The female guard searched through them and took away a cassette tape that they had overlooked back at the police station. Then she made me do the old "squat and cough" routine to make sure I wasn't concealing anything inside one of my orifices. After that I was allowed to put my clothes back on and was led to the large holding cell where I would spend the next day or so.

It was a twenty- by thirty-foot space that had beige school tiles on three walls. The fourth wall was made of prison bars. Near the front righthand corner of the cell was a shiny aluminum cubicle just big enough for a person and a toilet. There were skinny little benches lining the walls and spaced out in the middle of the floor, and on the left wall there were two pay phones.

Cathy, Helen, and I found a small space on one of the narrow benches in the middle of the cell. It was really way too small for three people to be sitting on, but we crammed ourselves there anyway. Most of the other forty or so women were sleeping, but a few were quietly talking and others were just staring into space.

Fluorescent lamps were shining down on us, and there were no windows to see out of. That didn't bother me at first, but as time went on, it began to have the Twilight Zone effect. I had no way of knowing if it was night or day, sunny or rainy . . . I lost all sense of time. We were only there for a day and a half, but after a while, if I looked at my watch and it said four o'clock, I couldn't be sure if it was a.m. or p.m.

The cell was also extremely hot. Before long, Helen and I moved to an empty piece of floor (most of it was covered by shoeless sleeping women). An elderly lady we dubbed Grandma, who was sitting across from us, made some room on the bench where she was sitting and Cathy stationed herself there.

It turned out that Grandma was there because someone knocked her packages out of her arms on her way home from the store and she hit him with her purse. For that, the poor old lady was arrested. She was there with us almost the whole time, and was very sweet although she mainly kept to herself. When feeding time came around, Grandma would give Helen the bread from her sandwiches, because Helen's a vegetarian, and couldn't eat the meat.

There was also an extremely big-busted lady in the cell with us (we're talking like Triple F here) who was lying on the floor near the bars. When we first arrived, she had popped up, her chest half falling out of her bustier-type top, and asked us why we were there.

We still weren't really sure, but they had told our parents that we were being charged with rioting, so that's what we told her. (She was in for prostitution.) She said that our being there was complete bullsh-t. Especially after she found out our ages (Cathy's 18, Helen and I are 16). That's basically the same response that we got from everyone: they all said it was bullsh-t, and that we were babies.

After that we chatted for a little while, and made phone calls home just to check in. We wanted to call our friends and stuff but it was like 5:30 on a Sunday morning. We decided to try to get some sleep. I don't know about Helen or Cathy, but I couldn't sleep a wink that night.

I spent the next twelve hours or so in the same cell befriending crackheads and prostitutes, and then it started to smell really bad and they moved us all to another cell. It wasn't until late Monday afternoon—almost forty-eight hours after we were arrested—that they took us out one by one and brought us through a long passageway. There I met my lawyer, a middle-aged Irish lady who was appointed by the court to represent me.

She said the whole thing was ridiculous and that I would be released but would probably have to come back and appear in court later on. They put me on a bench and I could see my mom sitting on the other side of the courtroom. I had to wait for around twenty minutes while they arraigned other people, but I couldn't understand a word of what they said.

Then they called my name and the prosecuting attorney asked for a "restraining order" to keep me out of the area covered by the 9th Precinct. The judge seemed kind of ticked off, like they were wasting his time (Helen and a couple of the others had already come before him). "Didn't we already go through this?" he asked. He said no to the restraining order, and announced a court date in January. Finally, I was allowed to go home.

In January, the court date was postponed because the police had not signed something called a deposition. We were given another date for March. At that hearing the charges were finally dropped because the police had failed to complete some type of paperwork within ninety days of the arrest.

When I tell people my story, one of the most commonly asked questions is, "Would you do the same thing if a similar situation came up?" I guess my answer should be no but it's not.

I would still stick up for my friend, which is all that I really did to begin with. I would try to watch my back a little bit more, and I probably wouldn't yell at a cop the way I did. But hey, what can I tell you? Everything that happened that night happened so fast that all I had to act on was gut instinct. I didn't have time to think about what I was doing, or the consequences of my actions. It all comes down to good ol' fight or flight, and I sure as hell wasn't going to run away and desert my friends.

I never really trusted the cops, not even as a small child, because of hearing about corrupt police on the nightly news. When my grandmother's store got ripped off and she needed their help, they never seemed to come through. The same thing goes for most of the people I know. Yet the police were always very good at harassing the homeless street peddlers that my grandmother would allow to set up shop outside her store.

In my early teens, the cops were more foes than friends to me. When I ran away from home, I always had to be on my guard so that I wouldn't get arrested. One time, I was sleeping in a storefront on St. Mark's Place with a bunch of my friends and was awakened at 6:30 in the morning by someone kicking me in the head. When I opened my eyes, I saw that it was a cop, who then told me to get my friends up and leave, which we did—very quickly.

That was also the summer the cops raided a peaceful squat on East 13th Street in Manhattan. I knew people who lived in those buildings and who were beaten and arrested for defending their homes.

After my arrest, whatever ability I might have had left to

someday respect the police is completely gone. I think there needs to be an almost complete revamping of our police force.

One of the problems is the mayor's crackdown on "quality of life" crimes. I don't feel cops should be allowed to hassle people for making too much noise, or drinking a beer on the sidewalk, when there are 6-year-old children being beaten and raped. We as a society have to look at the priorities that we set for the police force. I don't know about the rest of you, but not getting robbed, beaten, raped, or killed on my way home takes total priority over a harmless group of people drinking or blasting their radios.

The cops I've dealt with have been a very heavy-handed bunch of people. They forever pick on those who are rejected or cut off from mainstream society—like the poor and the young—because they know that society's throwaways have no political leverage. Most people won't care if one more teenager goes to jail for being a little rebellious, or another squatter gets forced out of her home.

Cops are also well aware of how to cover their tracks, what they can do to you and still be able to say that you brought it on yourself, or that it was an accident. Either way, they know they can't be held accountable for their actions.

Cops are often rude and derogatory too. More than once they've called me stupid, and when those cops made crude comments to us in the station house there was nothing that we could say or do to make them eat their words. We were in handcuffs in the middle of a police station.

I would love to know how we are supposed to feel safe in a city that is protected by people approaching middle age who beat the hell out of teenagers and sexually harass 16-year-old girls.

Some Serious Déjà Vu

War Stories

New York City Is Worlds Apart from El Salvador

By Norma E. López

My name is Norma. I came to the United States from El Salvador in 1985. In my country, I lived with my father, my mother, and my sister. Our house was big and had a garden. I was going to school, and was doing great in my classes. I had many friends. In El Salvador a lot of women don't work. My sister and I liked that because when we came home from school, we knew that our mother was waiting for us with hot lunch—and there was somebody to talk to.

A civil war was going on in El Salvador the whole time I was growing up, but in 1979 it started to affect more people. Everything changed. The schools were closed frequently, the people didn't work, food prices went up. Teachers were often on strike because the government didn't have the money to pay their salaries. El Salvador is a small country, so fights between the army and the guerrillas occurred everywhere. The army recruits boys to fight. And the guerrillas recruit both boys and girls. I had a friend who was killed after one year in the army when a bomb exploded in his helicopter. I felt sad for him. I knew him when I was a little girl. I know he had many goals for his future. That day his dreams ended.

Every day in my country many young people like my friend lose their dreams. Watching the TV news was horrible because I saw people suffering—crying for their dead relatives. One day I went to visit a friend who lived in an area where more intense fighting was taking place. When she came back from the supermarket, she said, "A group of men killed my friend because she gave food to guerrillas." I was so scared that I started crying. My friend said, "Don't cry. That happens every day." I was also crying for her because she lost her feeling. I felt that she was indifferent. When I came back to my house, I spoke with my mother about what happened. I said, "I don't want to be a monster without feeling."

My father's sister in New York sent money for our food because my father didn't have a job. One day my aunt called and said, "Brother, I am moving to California. I will send money for you and your family to come to the United States. I will leave my New York apartment for you." My father accepted her offer. I didn't want to move to New York. I thought of my friends, my teachers, my school. My parents told me that my life in the United States would be better. But that didn't make leaving any easier. I knew I probably couldn't come back to this country that was my home.

Life in New York was only better in some ways. Everybody spoke English and we couldn't understand them. My father worked as a cook and my mother was a baby-sitter. My sister and I went to our first day of school. We didn't like the subway noise and the crowds. But our classes weren't so difficult because they were bilingual. We had three English classes each day to learn English.

In high school, I discovered there were many racial problems. We didn't have these problems in El Salvador. My mother told me that a person's race or skin color doesn't matter. What matters is who that person is—her feelings, her manner. No one discriminated against me, but I saw fights in high school between Hispanics and Blacks, Dominicans and Puerto Ricans. Each group said, "We are the best."

I didn't know the word *racism* in Spanish. When I learned it, I didn't like it. I learned what the word meant in the Student Unity Club. Members of this club are against racism. They are from different countries. Each member talked about her culture. I think that racism deprives us of learning about different cultures.

Even though we weren't living in a country at war, in the United States our problems didn't end—my parents decided to get a divorce. I felt very sad. Very often I cried at night when everybody was sleeping. One night I said, "I don't want to cry anymore, I will talk to my parents, I will try to resolve the problem. If I can't resolve the problem, I will accept it." It took a lot of courage but I talked with my parents. My father said, "This is not your problem. I don't want you to interfere." I was so upset. I knew that this problem was affecting our family.

But I made a decision and said, "This is not my problem. My problem is to finish high school and think about my future plans." I feel satisfied with myself because I graduated high school this year. Then I was selected for the *New Youth Connections* Summer Journalism Workshop, which for me was very special. My future plans are to go to college, study hard, and do my best.

How My Family Escaped the Nazis

By Alison Stein Wellner

All of my life, I have been hearing about how my family escaped from the Nazis. The stories I've been told always begin in Cracow, Poland, in the early 1930s. Hankah (my grandmother) married Wilhelm, a handsome watchmaker. They lived in a good neighborhood right near their families. Hankah soon became pregnant, and gave birth to a daughter, Alina. Life was good for this Jewish family.

Hankah and Wilhelm didn't pay attention to the rise to power of a man named Adolf Hitler, the head of the Nazi party in neighboring Germany. He had a maniacal hatred of Jews. He believed that Jews caused all of the world's problems, and that they were a lower race, subhuman beings.

Then in 1939, the Nazis invaded Poland. Proclamations were made: All Jews must wear a yellow star. All male Jews must adopt the middle name Israel. All female Jews must adopt the middle name Sara. All Jews must have a J stamped on their passports and on their identity cards. Jews were no longer allowed to patronize "Aryan" stores, or allowed to use public facilities, like parks. They couldn't ride in trains, drive cars, or own bicycles. Life became increasingly difficult. Hankah and Wilhelm didn't know what to do.

Meanwhile, in utmost secrecy, the Nazis came up with the "Final Solution" to the "Jewish Question." They decided that all Jews must be eliminated. All Jews must die. In March of 1941, the Cracow ghetto was created. It was about ten New York City blocks long by five blocks wide with a brick wall around it and a barbed wire fence around the wall. Cracow's entire Jewish population—18,000 people—was forced to leave their homes and crammed into this space. Hankah and Wilhelm had to leave their nice house and go live in the ghetto. Five people had to fit in one room. This was not the life that they were used to.

Hankah and Wilhelm began to hear rumors. Rumors of awful places where they would be worked to death. Trapped in the ghetto, they were easy prey for the Nazis. Still, Hankah and Wilhelm did not want to just give up. They began to think about ways to escape. They knew that the best chance that they had for survival was to escape individually. They'd find each other somehow.

Wilhelm volunteered as a fireman. This work took him to areas outside the ghetto. That was how he escaped. With her husband gone, Hankah felt a sense of impending disaster. She had to get Alina out. She knew that the skinny 4-year-old girl would not have a chance in a work camp. In the dead of night, Hankah and her brother Zishue dropped Alina over the wall that surrounded the ghetto and she scrambled through a hole in the wire fence. Alina had a note attached to her coat, which asked whoever found her to shelter her. She ran crying into the night.

Hankah was now alone in the ghetto. There was no way out for her. She was trapped. Beginning in May 1942, Jews could no longer work outside the ghetto. Escape was thoroughly impossible. The "selections" (the Nazis' decisions about who would be transported to concentration camps) had started. Everyone would have to board the rickety cattle cars that would take them to hell. Hankah, her parents, brothers, and sisters stood on the long line, waiting to board the train.

Hankah was thinking how glad she was that Wilhelm and Alina had escaped, and prayed that they would find each other, somehow. A voice interrupted her thoughts. "Do you want to escape?" She turned around and stared at her cousin Fred. "How?" she asked quietly. "Don't ask questions. Come with me now. Leave your bag." Hankah began to call to her parents to follow, but Fred stopped her. "They won't make it. You can't say goodbye to them. We can't wait another second. Come on!" Hankah walked away with Fred. She didn't look back.

Hankah and Fred went down into the sewers. They began to move quickly, because it was only a matter of time before the Nazis realized that they were gone. After a little while, they heard noise behind them. Voices. And gunshots! "It's only a little farther," Fred called to Hankah. She didn't answer. Just as they climbed out, poison gas was released into the sewer. But they were out. They were free.

I don't know how they all found each other, but somehow Hankah, Wilhelm, and Alina were reunited. They changed their names, got new identification papers, and a new religion. They pretended to be devout Catholics. Hankah wore a big cross to prove it. Still, it was extremely dangerous for the family to stay in Poland. Since their escape, they had already been arrested and questioned. The Nazis had developed guidelines to determine a person's race. They measured people's heads and their noses to see if they were Jewish. But the Nazi guidelines, based more on stereotypes than science, were hardly foolproof. It was determined that Hankah, Wilhelm, and Alina were not a Jewish family.

Not wanting to take any chances, they moved to a different town, although they stayed in Poland. Wilhelm opened up a small jewelry store, and they tried to settle down to a normal life. But not for long. Since Wilhelm was a watchmaker, he knew how to deal with small parts. The Nazis wanted him to go to a work camp and make bombs. There was no way out. Hankah and Alina took Wilhelm down to the train station, where he joined a large group of men, under guard. Hankah took off her gold watch, put it in the guard's hand, and asked him to look the other way. Hankah and Alina waited. The guard didn't look away. It was too late.

Just then the air raid sirens went off, which meant that Allied bombers were flying into the area. Instead of going to the public air raid shelter, Hankah and Alina went back to their house, which wasn't that far from the station. When they went down to the basement, Wilhelm was there. Apparently, in all the confusion, Wilhelm managed to slip underneath the train, and escape after the train pulled out. It was just pure luck. But the family had to leave. The Nazis were sure to realize that he was missing and come after him.

The family took to the road again. There wasn't time to get new identification papers, so they had to travel by foot, for the most part, through the woods. They were planning to cross the border and make their way to Hungary. The Nazis hadn't invaded Hungary . . . yet. They settled in Hungary. After a few months the Germans came. The Nazis were dissatisfied with the way the Hungarians were treating the Jews (too nicely) and so they decided to start running things. Hankah was pregnant, but the family went on the road again, traveling in an open truck covered with fruit for most of their journey. They headed east. While they were on the road, the Nazis, who had been suffering severe losses, surrendered. Hitler was dead. They decided to head to Germany to try and locate their family. In Munich, Hankah had her baby, a little girl named Mira.

Mira is my mother. My grandparents (Hankah and Wilhelm) were very lucky to have survived. Few of their relatives did. Hankah's parents died in the Auschwitz concentration camp. They refused to eat the food they were given, because it wasn't kosher. Hankah's favorite sister, Regina, was killed by the Nazis. Upon arrival at Auschwitz, the Nazis took Regina's daughter to the gas chambers. She decided to die with her daughter. My grandmother's other siblings were also sent to Auschwitz. They survived.

Fred, Hankah's cousin who helped her escape from the ghetto, got himself out of many a bad situation. After he left the ghetto, he went to Hungary, where he was captured and placed in a work camp on a farm. Hungary was a good place to be captured, because the camps were run by Hungarians for the most part, not by Nazis. Security was lax. Fred built a shack in the woods, and began sneaking off to supply it with food. When the camp started to enforce tighter restrictions, he grabbed his girlfriend and her brother and they went to live in the woods.

It took the various family members three years to locate each other. They reunited in Germany but they no longer felt safe in Europe, even though the war was over and the Nazis had been defeated. They decided to move to America, to a place called the Bronx. Some of them didn't even feel safe in America, so they moved on to Israel, the newly formed Jewish state. My grandmother was haunted by her memories of the Holocaust until she died. I never knew my grandfather; he died before I was born.

I am proud and honored to come from a family of survivors. Stories like theirs have to be told, no matter how unpleasant, so the world won't forget, and it won't happen again.

My Escape from the Secret Police

By Hanify Ahmed

I was arrested when I was 16 but it's not what you think. In 1988 I was still living in Afghanistan, the country where I was born. The Soviet Union invaded my country in 1979. The Soviet army quickly took over the big cities and the government. Some Afghanis (natives of Afghanistan) cooperated with them and set up a new government under Soviet control. But many people fought back against the Soviet and the Afghani troops who supported the new government. I was one of those resisters.

The people of Mazar City, where I grew up, always opposed foreign control of my country. They have always supported the resistance fighters, commonly called the Mujahidin or Freedom Fighters. Even today the government controls Mazar City but the people do not support its rule. The young boys who help the Freedom Fighters form groups of six at the most. They are known as student groups. One student leads the group, determines who will be asked to join, and assigns the work. Back in

1988, when I was 14, I joined one of these groups. The members were my close friends so they trusted me, and asked me to help them.

I agreed to help and my resistance activities continued through 1988. I passed out newspapers published by the Freedom Fighters and placed notices in the public park. I passed out flyers warning civilians where the Mujahidin were going to ambush the government forces so innocent people wouldn't be there when the fighting started. Others collected money for the Freedom Fighters and passed information to them. Since it was so dangerous we never told anyone that we were part of this group, not even our families. If we were discovered by the government then our families wouldn't be blamed for knowing about us.

In November of 1988 my family went on an overnight visit to my uncle, who had been seriously injured by a government tank. I did not go to school the next day. When we returned home my neighbor, who was also a classmate, informed me that the other members of my student group had been taken from school that day by the government secret police. While my parents weren't sure if I had joined a student group, I told my mother what had happened to my friends because I was afraid of what was going to happen to me. When my father returned from work, my mother told him about the other students. My father took me to my grandmother's house because he knew the police would come to our house in search of me.

The next day my father told me that I would go with my mother, brother, and sisters to Kabul, the capital of Afghanistan. We went there to stay with my other grandmother. Several days later my father joined us. We rented a home in Kabul. My father decided to move to Kabul because it would be easier to hide there. At that time Freedom Fighters were launching fifteen to twenty-five rockets in Kabul each day and killing many civilians. No one would think that we would go there to hide. Also, people who were running away from the government were running to other countries and not staying in Afghanistan. That was why he felt we would be safe there.

I stayed in our house for almost one and a half years. My parents felt I would be safer if I stayed at home. I was afraid that if I went to school they would take me away like they took away my friends.

I went back to school in February of 1990. My father worked for the Ministry of Education, and he felt that the government was not paying as much attention to the students as they normally did because the fighting in and around Kabul was so bad. I attended school whenever it was open until August. This time I did not become involved with the students who worked for the resistance movement. But one day in August, two men came to my class. They were members of the secret police. I knew who they were because they were dressed like plainclothes cops and they were carrying guns. They asked if I was in the class, then they talked to the teacher in the doorway. The teacher told me to go with them.

I left the classroom with them and asked where we were going. They told me to be quiet and keep moving. We got into a car. I realized that we were going to the headquarters of the Khad (the secret police) because when we reached the checkpoints they only had to show their identification cards to get through without being searched. The car stopped in front of a house. There were three or four men outside and there were electric wires on the outside of the walls so no one could escape. The two men showed their identification, and we passed through. They took me to a room in the basement. They left me alone and locked the door.

The room was like a cell. I was very afraid. What was going to happen to me? I'm not sure how much time passed but sometime later the two men returned with another man who appeared to be their boss. They told me that they knew who I was because the students from my group in Mazar had told them about me. They kept asking for my name and about my activities in Mazar. They also asked me if my father knew of my activities. They said that if I did not give them the information, they would beat me, and take me to the Central Jail. I was very afraid of going to the

Central Jail because everyone knows that if you are taken there, you disappear forever. The questioning continued for perhaps ninety minutes and I tried to hold back as much information as I could. Then they left me in the room by myself for the rest of the night.

The next morning they all came back and asked the same questions. They also asked me what political party I belonged to and why I had passed the newspapers out. They continued to frighten me by asking me if I knew what the government did with people who were involved in resistance activities. The questioning again lasted for about ninety minutes. Then they left. When they returned they prepared to move me. I thought they were going to take me to the Central Jail. We left the headquarters, and they put me in the car. They said nothing to me. They drove to an area near my house, and told me to get out of the car. I was free.

My entire family was at the house when I arrived. My father told me that when I did not come home from school, he went to my school to see what happened. The school officials told him that I had been taken by the secret police. My father bribed the secret police by giving them his car to get me released. They told him that they would destroy my arrest papers but I would have to leave because they would come for me again.

My father took me to a friend's home. My father talked with his friend, Mamood, for about two hours in one room while I waited in another. My father came to me, and hugged me good-bye and told me to be careful. He left the house telling me to do whatever Mamood told me to do. That night I stayed with Mamood. He told me that we were going to take the bus from Kabul to the city of Lugar. He told me that if any soldiers stopped us we should say that we were going to Lugar for a wedding party.

In Lugar, Mamood arranged with the Freedom Fighters to have me taken to Peshawar City in Pakistan, a country bordering Afghanistan. He hugged me, told me to be good, and told me not to go too far from the group because there were land mines out there that would hurt me. He told me that they would take me somewhere in Pakistan where people would take care of me. The journey to Pakistan took two days. We traveled at night for fear of being caught by the government forces. When we arrived in Pakistan the group broke up, but one member of the group took me to a house.

When I arrived at the house, Khodadad, the older brother of one of my resistance group's members, was there. He told me that I alone of the six had escaped. None of the others had been heard from since they were taken from school. He told me that he knew who I was from his brother and that he would help me. He said I wasn't safe in either Afghanistan or Pakistan. Khodadad took me to a house for the Freedom Fighters, and told me to stay inside because people had disappeared after they left the house. I stayed in the house until the night they took me to the airport, and sent me to the United States. That was six months ago.

When I left Afghanistan I was not thinking of leaving my country for good. I wanted to get away from the secret police, the bombs, and the missiles. But I am afraid to go back because I am afraid of what the government will do to me. I am afraid if I go back, I will disappear like my friends have disappeared. If I return to Afghanistan, I will unquestionably face persecution due to my involvement in student activities.

I have been living with my cousin since I came here, and am attending International High School now. I hope to remain safe, and continue my education. I still believe that Afghanistan should be governed by the people through free elections. The struggle in Afghanistan will continue as long as the government now in power is ruling the country.

The L.A. Riots: Beirut All Over Again

By Mohamad Bazzi

One image of the Los Angeles riots I will never forget is a picture I saw in the newspaper of a stripped, burned-out car sitting in the haze in the middle of a desolate avenue. As soon as I saw it, I felt numb. I heard the gunshots, sensed the terror. For a moment I was back on the streets of my native Beirut.

The scene reminded me of Al-Shayah, the inner-city Lebanese neighborhood where I grew up. My block was on a busy street, by Beirut standards. It was also a favorite target of trigger-happy Christian militia snipers. When gunfire erupted—sometimes killing innocent bystanders—everyone would run for cover, leaving the whole street deserted, dead.

I lived a few hundred feet from the "green line," an invisible but lethal marker that divided the Christian East and Muslim West sectors of Beirut for more than fifteen years. Back in 1943, when the Lebanese people achieved independence from France, the departing French set up a plan to ensure that Muslims and

Christians got equal representation in the new government. But in practice, their plan proved unfair and divisive, and contributed to the outbreak of civil war.

Christians, who made up a slight majority at the time, got most of the money and power. A few Muslims managed to prosper and join the ranks of the middle and upper classes, but many more were shut out by the green lines. In 1975, after decades of unemployment, crumbling schools, rampant poverty, and a general atmosphere of frustration and hopelessness, the poor finally took to the streets. They've been there ever since.

See any similarities? I do.

In a way, Los Angeles has its own green line. It is a border that separates South Central and other neighborhoods like it from mainstream America, and it's patrolled by L.A.P.D. snipers. The people of South Central Los Angeles and the people of West Beirut have a great deal in common. Both are minorities, both are alienated. The Muslims of West Beirut, like L.A.'s Blacks and Latinos, have long been excluded from the national political and economic life. In both places the inequities were built into the system from the beginning.

Many of those who have been doing the fighting in Lebanon for so long are just like me—young men between the ages of 16 and 25, reared in neighborhoods like Al-Shayah. We have wrestled with the same problems that led our American counterparts to set L.A. ablaze: lack of job opportunities, inadequate schools, and a system that doesn't work for us. In Beirut, as in L.A., young men have resorted to crime and violence. Gangs thrive in both worlds. In L.A. they have names like Crips and Bloods. In Lebanon they take forms like the Hezbollah—the Shiite Muslim Party of God. For nearly twenty years, young men have formed the backbone of most of these groups. To this day, the neighborhood militia still offers Lebanese youth their most lucrative job opportunities.

The city of Beirut lies in ruins. Those buildings that haven't been completely bombed out are scarred by bullet holes. Most families have lost loved ones in the fighting. Is Los Angeles destined to become an American Beirut? Is New York? Atlanta? Not if the powers that be heed Los Angeles Mayor Tom Bradley's call for "economic empowerment" for young minority men. Not if they work to bring inner-city schools back to life and fully address the other roots of urban poverty and injustice. Otherwise, I and others who came to this country after experiencing the terrors of Beirut are in for some serious déjà vu.

Operation Paintball: Splattering the Enemy

By Julio Pagan

I've been running away from the guys who are chasing me for five minutes. My adrenaline is flowing and it keeps me alert. I see them in the distance and run up a hill to get away. They spot me. Shots ring out.

I use the communication link in my helmet to call for help but I'm too far away and the damned thing can't reach anybody. My mind tells me to run into the clearing and face the skirmish, but my fear of getting shot tells me to run down the opposite side of the hill and hide in the tall grass.

I listen to my fear and hide. I can hear them talking as they walk toward me. In a desperate attempt to escape, I get up and run toward a nearby river. I hear more shots. One hits me in the back and the other hits my leg. I fall to the ground and my heartbeat slows down. I lie frozen on the ground for a while, staring at my attackers as they walk away laughing. Red liquid seeps through my shirt. Even though I've taken a hit, I'm feeling great. I stand up, thinking, "I love paintball!"

Paintball is a game in which you hunt people down with a high-tech air-based gun that shoots a marble-like ball filled with paint. The object of the game is either to capture your enemy's flag or to eliminate as many members of the opposing team as you can without getting hit yourself.

During the game you can express all your hostility and anger by pumping a couple of paintballs into your opponent's chest and eliminating him. It's the closest you can get to fighting a war without anyone getting hurt. Some people play to win money in major tournaments, some do it to release tensions, and others, like me, just do it for fun.

I got my first taste of paintball when I was about 14 and saw a copy of *Action Pursuit Games* magazine at the local candy store. The cover showed two guys with these weird helmets and guns surrounded by bright blots of color. I opened it up and saw more guns, helmets, and other special gear. "This is great," I thought. "Just like in the military." I'd been in the Marine cadets and in the Royal Rangers at my church and I thought this game would provide a great opportunity to use my training.

The only problem was that I didn't see any young people in the pictures. Was there some reason why teenagers couldn't play paintball? I turned to the last page of the magazine to see when the next issue was coming out and saw these words: "New Column: Kids' paint, starting next month." All right!

I told all my friends about my discovery and they loved the idea. We talked about it for hours. Finally, someone asked how much the guns cost. That was our stumbling block. The price range for these guns (they have all types, from .357 magnum revolvers to rifles and semiautomatics) was anywhere from $79 to $700. Where were we supposed to get that much money?

We decided to buy a plastic version called Gotcha, which only cost $30 a pair. We quickly found out why they were so cheap. They had a shooting range of only ten feet and shot these little bullet-shaped paint capsules that were hardly noticeable upon impact. But it was a start. We enjoyed playing with these at our neighborhood park. The main drawback was all the running we had to do—you had to get really close to your target to make a hit.

After a while, we upgraded our weaponry to the lowest-priced "real" paintgun. It was called Splat Master. We thought this gun would be the answer to our prayers. It was air-based and shot real paintballs, not little pellets. The range for the Splat Master was about thirty feet, so it easily eliminated all the running. But then we got bored with having to constantly reload the gun (it only held ten paintballs at a time) and decided to upgrade again. We saved all our allowance, birthday, and Christmas money and bought even better models. This time each of us got something different. I bought the Razorback, a pump-action gun with a maximum range of about 200 feet, for $169.

By now, I was an avid player in search of new challenges. One of my friends got his driver's license and we started traveling to regulation paintball fields on Long Island and in New Jersey for organized games with other paintball fans. We played on fields that were as long as three football fields and had hills, streams, and other natural obstacles. The teams had between 150 and 200 people and the games lasted all weekend.

There are a lot of reasons why my friends and I love paintball. It's more of a physical challenge than football (my second favorite sport) and it offers a mental challenge too. You're always trying to stay one step ahead of your opponents—running, jumping, hiding, and thinking what to do next. It's like hunting, only better, because you're hunting and being hunted at the same time. And it's good practice for people going into the military or law enforcement (something my friends and I are planning to do).

Unfortunately, there are some Rambo types who don't realize that paintball is just a game. Some people will show up at the field with knives and machetes, but the referees take these weapons away from them at the entrance and make sure that no real guns enter the field. Another problem is that some people might carry their "battlefield" attitudes into the street. They might use their paintball guns outside of a field, which could be dangerous. People like that give paintball a bad name.

But if you're mature enough to know the difference between a game and real life, you can have a great time with paintball. It feels good when you make your first hit, it's like hitting your first home run or making your first touchdown. Try it, you just might like it.

My Summer in the Israeli Army

By Melissa Chapman

The summer of 1989 was a major turning point in my life. I spent six weeks in Israel training with the Israeli army. I had enrolled in a program called Chetz Vakeshet (Bow and Arrow), which trains Jewish teenagers in the skills and practices of the Israeli army.

I had been to Israel three years before, to visit my sister, who was studying there. I'd also studied the Jewish faith and culture for ten years at a private religious school in Brooklyn. But before my summer at Chetz Vakeshet, my connection to Israel was merely the memorization of abstract facts. My tour with the army let me experience Israel from an entirely new perspective.

The morning after I arrived, I was awakened at dawn and told I had fifteen minutes to be outside with the rest of my squad. I scrambled out of bed, my back aching from a sleepless night on a hard cot. I could barely keep my eyes open as my samal (captain) launched us into an hourlong session of nonstop, high-impact calisthenics. By the time we finished exercising, I was famished. But instead of heading straight to the dining hall, I got my second taste of army discipline. We had to line up, in perfectly straight rows, and form a half square around our superiors. We remained in these positions until each squad entered the dining hall in a synchronized march.

Little did I know that these living conditions were to be the most luxurious I'd experience for the rest of the tour. These first few days gave us a chance to get acquainted in a semirelaxed atmosphere, compared with what came next—the most physically challenging adventure of my life.

At the beginning of the next week, we loaded our belongings on a bus and traveled to an army base in the Negev Desert. We had to lug all our belongings and pitch our own tents, sleep on army cots, eat in the mess hall (including setting up, cooking, and washing the dishes), and train alongside the soldiers at the base. We learned to handle M-16 machine guns and follow obstacle courses. Every night at 11:30, I fell into bed like a dead weight. It was a complete change from anything I'd ever done. I wasn't used to pushing myself so hard. During my first free weekend, I was so exhausted that I slept about eighteen hours.

But the hardest part of my training was when I went to the firing range. I had to lie down on my stomach and position the gun on my shoulder while aiming at the target. It was one of the most terrifying experiences in my life, knowing that I had the power of life and death in my hands. I finally understood what a soldier must overcome in learning to put his feelings aside and focus on fighting the enemy, even if that means killing someone. The experience made me acutely aware of the different ways in which Israeli Jews and American Jews are brought up. In Israel, all Jews are required to join the army at age 18. A basic part of living there is knowing you will have to put your life at risk to ensure the perpetuation of a Jewish homeland. Even Israeli teens who share my reservations about handling guns cannot choose not to use them.

During the first few weeks of the trip, all the activity had strengthened my physical discipline, but it had no spiritual effect on me. That changed when we went to climb Masada, a huge mountain where a wealthy and advanced Jewish city had been built thousands of years ago. That city was eventually invaded and destroyed. We set out at 2 a.m. so we could reach the top by sunrise. We all camped out in our sleeping bags at the bottom of the mountain and tried to get a little rest. When I awoke it was pitch black outside, and each person had to hold a fire-lit torch to help light the dirt path up the mountain. I'm not sure exactly what happened inside me, but when I finally reached the top of Masada, I was overtaken with this complete sense of peace.

Walking among the ruins, I was actually witnessing a place where thousands of years ago, my ancestors had thrived and built an empire. We'd finally conquered back our land and were continuing where they'd left off. As I looked around at the other members of my group, I felt a renewed sense of unity with them. We were the next Jewish generation, and the fate of Israel was in our hands.

The ultimate test of my physical and emotional discipline came during the fourth week of my training. We embarked on a three-day hike, which began in northern Israel, near the Kziv River, and ended at the Kinereth Sea. All the while we traveled by foot, through fields and streams and over steep mountains. Every night we slept outside in tents and ate canned army food (or whatever wild fruit we could find along the way). It was really hard in the beginning. We were fatigued from the never-ending hiking, the tasteless canned food and the tension of constantly being together. We were grating on each other's nerves. I was beginning to think I was a full-fledged masochist, and I just wanted to get back to my cozy room in Brooklyn and go to sleep. I pretty much wanted to kill everyone in my squad.

Then we began a five-hour hike in the hot midday sun, up a very steep and narrow mountain. Somehow we managed to reach the top, with each person helping and watching out for the others. It was the climax of my trip. I had pushed myself to my outermost limits. I also learned the value of cooperating with others to achieve something I could never have done on my own. Chetz Vakeshet gave me the chance to get reacquainted with my heritage and, in a way, to experience what my forefathers had thousands of years ago, when they traveled through Israel by foot. For me, it was like reliving history.

Letter to an Iraqi Mother and Other Student Reactions to the Gulf War

To an Iraqi mother,

I'm sure the last piece of mail you would want to receive is from an American, even an American who is a friend. I don't know if you've lost a child or not, but I assume the devastation the U.S. has made the people of Iraq suffer through is enough to cause you great pain. I can't speak for the U.S. government, but I can apologize personally for the U.S. aggression. Apologies are probably the last thing you want to hear, since they don't do you or me any good, but that's all I have to offer.

Sheila Maldonado

Although death is a huge price to pay to ensure the freedom of others, I feel a strong sense of pride in our troops for committing themselves to such a noble cause. I only hope that this war can serve as a constant reminder to the rest of the world that no human being's right to freedom can be compromised. I'm not saying that war is the only way to eradicate dictators like Hussein. Unfortunately more humane approaches were unsuccessful this time and immediate military action was necessary.

I'm not sure what will come from Iraq's defeat. I feel euphoric yet at the same time skeptical. I wonder if this war can somehow prevent other powerful countries from following Iraq's example. Will it be the start of a new world order, one whose main objective is to ensure democracy for all people? Or is it just another war that the U.S. has involved itself in, only to be repeated when the next Hussein rises to power? Was it worth putting American lives in jeopardy only to have a repeat performance by some other avaricious dictator?

Freedom has never come easy or without some form of sacrifice. Maybe this war can effect a change in world affairs, and bring about a new beginning. Perhaps, for once, history will not repeat itself.

Melissa Chapman

Dear President Bush,

I hope if I ever become President of the United States I would make the same choice you made. You picked the right time to start the ground war. You didn't doubt our victory.

When my uncle came home from the war I asked him if the Gulf War was anything like the war in the South Bronx. He said they were alike because the drug dealers are hunting for land to sell their drugs.

What I'm trying to say is that to let kids like me and my schoolmates grow up in an environment full of drugs, rapes, and killings is like sending us to war. Even though we are too young to enlist, when we were born we enlisted in a lifetime war zone.

Keith Cruz

Dear Saddam Hussein,

Listen Mr. Hussein, why don't you come and live in America and stop all that messing around you're doing over there with the guns and people's lives and the environment. You could probably get on Social Security disability because you are crippled in your mind and then maybe you could qualify for a nursing home where you could play in a sandbox with little tanks and things. Or maybe you could go to Hollywood and make a billion dollars with *Saddam Hussein: the Movie, Return of S.H., Return of S.H. Part II, Return of S.H. Part III,* etc. Or maybe you could become a capitalist and make Hussein Mace Spray or Hussein Instant Death in a spray can (without fluorocarbons, of course).

Or you could build a resort in one of the desert states and call it Saddam's Bunker Away from Home. You know, a nice quiet place to run away from it all. If these sound too dull for you, you could ride the New York subways, say around 2 a.m. on any Saturday night. I'll pay your fare.

Theresa Bayer

Dear President Bush:

Our only stake in the liberation of Kuwait was oil. I ask you, Mr. President, is oil so precious that it is worth American lives? I don't think so.

How can you with a clear conscience even think of forcing Iraq out of Kuwait when the White South African government still enforces apartheid in South Africa? Why aren't American and allied forces trying to liberate Johannesburg?

I see you are ready to go to war over oil but not over the right to live in freedom. You are all for democracy but not for South Africans. With all due respect, you and your administration are a bunch of hypocrites.

Josie Bradley

Dear Iraqi Pen Pal,

I am a senior in high school and also a concerned citizen of the United States. Many students in the U.S. were protesting the war not solely for the benefit of America and the allied forces, but also to protect the people of Iraq. We sympathize with your people because we devastated your country. You felt the bombings and killings that we in the U.S. only saw on television. Our hearts go out to you and your people. We are all victims of this senseless war. Now that it is over, you are in our prayers.

Lindsey Williams

Dear Iraqi Teenager,

I have nothing but peaceful wishes in my heart toward all people. We need to look at each other as individuals. It would be a shame for our people to claim that we hate each other when we really don't know one another. I oppose people who are oppressive and abuse human rights. I dislike people who are prejudiced or think themselves superior because of their color, sex, or religion.

The war could perhaps have been avoided if we did not prejudge each other. Or maybe if we were not so imperialistic and greedy in taking over territory. Do you not have a vision of a world where we do something positive for the human race? We are the youth of the world. We do not have to perpetuate old prejudices.

Irma Millichip

The Price of War

Bombing City Schools

One Patriot missile fired: $600,000
One year of Board of Ed. Saturday
SAT review courses: $368,907

One jet: $25,000,000
High school drug abuse program for five years: $27,371,850

Daily fuel bill during air war: $10,000,000
Library books for high schools for five years: $9,857,562

Building one Stealth bomber: $530,000,000
Salaries of all high school academic teachers, 1989–90:
$525,814,000

Long-term care and compensation
for 6,000 American casualties: $2,000,000,000
Annual budget for School Food and Nutrition Services:
$205,535,422

One ground-to-ground missile fired: $100,000
Salaries for two school librarians, 1989–90:
$85,237

Sources: Military figures: New York Newsday *and Council on Economic Priorities. Board of Education figures:* Budget Estimate for Fiscal Year 1990–1991, New York City Board of Education, *volumes 1 and 2.*

No Parades for One Bronx Family

By Sheila Maldonado

Over the past few months, the pain of war reached out beyond the battlefield and found its way into the smallest corners of America. One of them was a fourth-floor walkup on Beck Street in the South Bronx. On January 29, Marine Corporal Ismael Cotto Jr. was killed in combat in Khafji, Saudi Arabia, 5,000 miles away from the streets where he grew up. "For [the government] not many have died," said his mother, Carmen Cotto, holding back her tears, "but when just one person dies that's a lot. The family is devastated."

Ismael Cotto was the ideal recruit. As a child, his mother remembers he loved to play with *juguetitos de soldado*, little toy soldiers. "He had a ton of them," she recalled. He and his brother Carlos were also members of the Cadets, a military version of the Boy Scouts. But Ismael seemed to take it more seriously than the rest. "We all went so far," Carlos explained, "but he went all the way . . . it was in his blood."

Martin Schiff, the brothers' wrestling coach at Alfred E. Smith High School, remembers Ismael for his determination to succeed. "He was tough and brave," he said. "Even if the other wrestler was bigger and stronger than he was, he was ready to go in and fight." Schiff said he was reliable as well. "He was like an assistant coach—like an adult." Besides that, Cotto was smart. "Students like Ismael come along every hundred years," exclaimed Frank Messina, his architectural drafting teacher at Smith. "In the sixteen years that I taught, I gave [only] two 100s. I gave Ismael one of them.... We tend to stereotype kids from the South Bronx," he continued, "but Ismael and his classmates had a future."

While the two brothers were in high school, Carlos said army recruiters "would come around practically every day" and try to shape those futures. "[Once] I had this recruiter bothering me," he recalled, "[and] I went in and failed [the test] on purpose so that he would leave me alone." Carlos said the recruiter told him he could take the test over and assured him he'd do better the second time around. "They'll do any little thing to get you in," he explained. "[They're] just salesmen."

At 18, when he graduated from high school, Ismael was ready to enlist but his mother talked him out of it. Instead, he went to City College to study computers and worked as a counselor for young people in his neighborhood. Three years later, in his junior year, he entered the Marines. "It was the way we were living—the way we grew up," recalled Carlos, "[Ismael] got tired of seeing the crime and the drugs and the teen pregnancies and the dropouts.... The military was offering him a chance to see the world outside the Bronx."

The other big reason was his career. Ismael hoped to work with computers in the military. "He went into the Marines to continue his studies," said his mother, "so he could have a trade that would support him later on." According to Carlos, the training Ismael was offered by his recruiter turned out to be an "empty promise." He was put on a waiting list, and placed in the infantry. "He was in a vehicle that battles tanks ... a guy of his intellect . . . he wanted to be an officer . . . he wanted to study." In his six and a half years in the Marines, Ismael Cotto never touched a computer.

He did get to travel, however, but not quite the way he pictured it. From a military base in North Carolina, he was transferred to California, where he met his future wife, Maria. In August of 1989, they shipped him to Japan for a full year of duty. "He wasn't allowed to bring his wife or daughter," said his brother. "He had no say in it. He tried to get out of it . . . [but] they wouldn't listen, they didn't care."

When Ismael finally returned to the U.S. last July, he had two months with his family before being shipped out again, this time to the Persian Gulf, this time for good. "[When you enlist] you're signing your life away," said Carlos. From Saudi Arabia, Ismael wrote to his mother "at least once a week." In his last letter, "He told me that his vehicle had broken down, it broke down all the time," she said. "They really suffered . . . they'd go four, five days in the same clothes, without washing . . . they walked from place to place in the heat, and when night came they'd stay right there in the sand."

Carlos spoke to his brother on the phone a few days before the war started in January. He said he sounded "very down." Carlos asked him if he needed anything. "Just a one-way ticket outta here," he replied. By that time, the military life had lost its glamour for Ismael. Carlos pointed to a picture on the wall in which his brother sports a white military cap, and a dark, pressed, navy blue uniform. He explained that the "dress blues" uniform that Marines wear in their official photos, "the one with the shiny buttons you see in all the ads," have to be paid for. It doesn't just come with the job. Ismael had to borrow one to have the picture taken.

"The attraction [the military holds for young people] is based on something that is mainly false," Carlos went on. "They only show you the glamour part. They don't remind you when you sign up . . . that you may be giving up your life."

For the Cotto family, there remain many questions about the

way Ismael died. At first, Marines visited their home and told them he had been killed by fire from allied troops ("friendly fire"). "They said it was an accident," said his mother, "Then they changed their story [and said it was the Iraqis]. I'd really like to know how it happened." Carlos explained that most of the information they have gotten has been from news reports. "They told us they'd get back to us [but] they never called back."

"For them, practically nobody died," said Ismael's mother. A single death, however, has left her family reeling with confusion, angry and disillusioned. She said, to her, the war was nothing more than a "whim" on the part of President Bush. "[It] could have been avoided," added Carlos. "My brother died in vain."

José Belén, a junior at Alfred E. Smith High School, where the Cotto brothers went to school, commented that while some may see it as a victory, they are forgetting families like the Cottos. The Persian Gulf War was certainly no victory to them. "We feel that throwing parades is a slap in the face," said Carlos. The Cottos feel they have nothing to celebrate. They can only mourn.

"It could have been me," reflected Mario Caraballo, another junior at Alfred E. Smith. "I wanted to be a pilot in the army," he said, "[but, now] I don't know." Carmen Cotto would like to warn young people like José and Mario against making the same mistake her son made: "Don't let yourself be blinded by all the pretty stuff they advertise in the army. Study hard, you can achieve anything you want by studying. You don't have to enlist."

In the end, Ismael Cotto did achieve a small portion of the glory he was promised as a young man. The Marines gave him his "dress blues" after all—the one with the shiny buttons. He wore it to his funeral. Instead of paying in cash, he paid for it with his life.

Except where otherwise noted, the stories in this book originally appeared in the following editions of *New Youth Connections:*

"When Things Get Hectic" by Juan Azize, April 1994

"What Happened to My American Dream?" by Natalie Neptune, September/October 1997

"My Abused Friend: She Needs More Help Than I Can Give" by Myriam Skye Holly, September/October and November 1994

"Home Is Where the Hurt Is" by Zeena Bhattacharya, September/October and November 1993

"My Terrible Secret: Breaking the Silence" by Anonymous, April 1991

"No One Spoke Up for Irma" by Ana Angélica Pines, September/October 1996

"A Proud Moment: Reporting the Abuse Upstairs" by Jessica Cabassa, May/June 1997

"Will There Ever Be Justice for David?" by Grismaldy Laboy, November and December 1996

"Maribel Feliciano: She Died in the Arms of a Friend" by Adrian Jefferson, December 1991

"His Sneakers, My Dreams" by Suzanne Joblonski, November 1990

"Remembering Mike" by Carlos Lavezzari, May 1992

"No One Deserves to Die Like That" by Wunika Hicks, April 1997

"How I Made Peace with the Past" by Paula M. Verma, *Foster Care Youth United,* May/June 1995

"Why I Love Gangsta Rap" by J. Slade Anderson, May 1993

"Women Are Under a Rap Attack" by Yelena Dynnikov, September/October 1992

"Diving into the Pit: I Came, I Saw, I Moshed" by Allen Francis, November 1994

"Gaybashers: What Are They Trying to Prove?" by Meliska Gruenler, May 1992

"The Media War Against Arabs" by Mohamad Bazzi, April 1993

"Violent Times, Violent Movies" by Daniel Jean-Baptiste, May 1992

"Hoods n' the Boys" by Karina Sang-Petrillo, May 1992

"We Wanted Revenge" by Carlos López, November 1990

"A Proud Moment: Turning In a Killer" by Anonymous, May/June 1997

"Why I Carry a Gun" by Anonymous, April 1992

"Why I Don't Have a Gun" by Anonymous, April 1994

"I Carry Mace . . . Just in Case" by Anonymous, April 1994

"My Secret Habit" by Anonymous, September/October 1992

"I Hated Myself" by David Miranda, April, May, and June 1993

"Racking, Bombing, Tagging . . . My Career as a *Writer*" by Anonymous, December 1992

"No More Clubbing for Me" by Fabayo McIntosh, September/October 1995

"Karate Killed the Monster in Me" by Robin K. Chan, November 1996

"Tired of Being a Target" by Loretta Chan, September/October 1993

"Why Guys Talk Nasty" by Nanci S. Paltrowitz, January/February 1994

"Tell Him Why" by Lisa Frederick, May 1992

"I Paid a High Price for Love" by Melissa Krolewski, November 1996

"He Won't Stop Hitting Me" by Anonymous, May 1992

"Dream Guy, Nightmare Experience" by Anonymous, January/February 1991

"My Love, My Friend, My Enemy" by Anonymous, September/October, November, and December 1991 and January/February 1992

"I Never Thought He'd Try to Kill Me" by Anonymous, December 1988

"The Anger Can Go Somewhere Else" by Anonymous, *Strange Brew,* a publication of the Urban Academy, April 1992

"Cops and Kids" reported by Julio A. Garcia, September/October 1995

"Caught in the Act" by Rance Scully, September/October 1995

"Rikers: Frontin' for Respect" by José R., *Streams 6,* a publication of the Waterways Project, 393 St. Pauls Avenue, Staten Island, New York 10304. Reprinted by permission.

"Busted" by Ligeia Minetta, May/June 1997

"New York City Is Worlds Apart from El Salvador" by Norma E. López, September/October 1989

"How My Family Escaped the Nazis" by Alison Stein Wellner, December 1992

"My Escape from the Secret Police" by Hanify Ahmed, May 1991

"The L.A. Riots: Beirut All Over Again" by Mohamad Bazzi, June 1992

"Operation Paintball: Splattering the Enemy" by Julio Pagan, January/February 1993

"My Summer in the Israeli Army" by Melissa Chapman, November 1991

"No Parades for One Bronx Family" by Sheila Maldonado, April 1991

Guide to Essays

Abortion

My Love, My Friend, My Enemy
185

Abuse

In Relationships

He Won't Stop Hitting Me 177
I Never Thought He'd Try to Kill
Me 196
I Paid a High Price for Love 171

In the Home

Home Is Where the Hurt Is 41
Letters to Parents 33
My Abused Friend: She Needs More
Help Than I Can Give 35
No One Spoke Up for Irma 53
A Proud Moment: Reporting the
Abuse Upstairs 59

Of a Sexual Nature

My Terrible Secret: Breaking the
Silence 49

African-Americans

Diving into the Pit: I Came, I Saw,
I Moshed 94
Tell Him Why 164
What Happened to My American
Dream? 26
Why I Love Gangsta Rap 89

AIDS

How I Made Peace with the Past
82

Alcohol/Substance Abuse

The Anger Can Go Somewhere
Else 202
How I Made Peace with the Past
82
I Never Thought He'd Try to Kill
Me 196
Letters to Parents 113
No More Clubbing for Me 146
Violent Times, Violent Movies
105

Arab-Americans
The Media War Against Arabs 102

Asian-Americans
Home Is Where the Hurt Is 41
Karate Killed the Monster in Me 149
My Escape from the Secret Police
    241
Tired of Being a Target 157

Caribbean-Americans
Caught in the Act 214
My Terrible Secret: Breaking the
    Silence 49
What Happened to My American
    Dream? 26

Death and Loss
His Sneakers, My Dreams 75
How I Made Peace with the Past
    82
Maribel Feliciano: She Died in the
    Arms of a Friend 72
No One Deserves to Die Like
    That 79
Remembering Mike 77
Will There Ever Be Justice for
    David? 63

Eating Disorders
My Secret Habit 128

Entertainment
Diving into the Pit: I Came, I Saw,
    I Moshed 94
No More Clubbing for Me 146
Operation Paintball: Splattering the
    Enemy 249
Racking, Bombing, Tagging . . .
    My Career as a *Writer* 141

Violent Times, Violent Movies
    105
Why I Love Gangsta Rap 89
Women Are Under a Rap Attack 91

Foreign Wars
How My Family Escaped the
    Nazis 236
The L.A. Riots: Beirut All Over
    Again 246
Letter to an Iraqi Mother and
    Other Student Reactions to the
    Gulf War 257
My Escape from the Secret Police
    241
My Summer in the Israeli Army 253
New York City Is Worlds Apart
    from El Salvador 233
No Parades for One Bronx Family
    263
The Price of War 261

Gays and Lesbians
Gaybashers: What Are They Trying
    to Prove? 99
I Hated Myself 132

Gun Violence
His Sneakers, My Dreams 75
No One Deserves to Die Like
    That 79
Remembering Mike 77
When Things Get Hectic 21
Why I Carry a Gun 119
Why I Don't Have a Gun 122
Will There Ever Be Justice for
    David? 63

Hispanic-Americans
I Hated Myself 132

My Love, My Friend, My Enemy 185

New York City Is Worlds Apart from El Salvador 233

No One Spoke Up for Irma 53

Will There Ever Be Justice for David? 63

Immigrants

Caught in the Act 214

How My Family Escaped the Nazis 236

The L.A. Riots: Beirut All Over Again 246

New York City Is Worlds Apart from El Salvador 233

What Happened to My American Dream? 26

Jewish-Americans

How My Family Escaped the Nazis 236

My Summer in the Israeli Army 253

Loyalty

Maribel Feliciano: She Died in the Arms of a Friend 72

My Abused Friend: She Needs More Help Than I Can Give 35

A Proud Moment: Turning In a Killer 117

We Wanted Revenge 115

When Things Get Hectic 21

Media

Gaybashers: What Are They Trying to Prove? 99

The Media War Against Arabs 102

Violent Times, Violent Movies 105

Parent-Child Relations

Home Is Where the Hurt Is 41

How I Made Peace with the Past 82

I Carry Mace . . . Just in Case 125

I Hated Myself 132

Letters to Parents 33, 113, 169

My Abused Friend: She Needs More Help Than I Can Give 35

My Love, My Friend, My Enemy 185

Tired of Being a Target 157

Peer Pressure

The Anger Can Go Somewhere Else 202

Gaybashers: What Are They Trying to Prove? 99

Hoods n' the Boys 108

I Hated Myself 132

We Wanted Revenge 115

Police Brutality/Misconduct

Busted 220

Caught in the Act 214

Cops and Kids 210

Reaction to the Anthony Baez Verdict 207

Will There Ever Be Justice for David? 63

Popular Music

Diving into the Pit: I Came, I Saw, I Moshed 94

No One Deserves to Die Like That 79

Why I Love Gangsta Rap 89

Women Are Under a Rap Attack 91

Prisons/Criminal Justice

Busted 220

Prisons/Criminal Justice (contd.)
Rikers: Frontin' for Respect 216
Will There Ever Be Justice for
    David? 63

Race Relations
How My Family Escaped the
    Nazis 236
Karate Killed the Monster in Me 149
The L.A. Riots: Beirut All Over
    Again 246
The Media War Against Arabs 102
New York City Is Worlds Apart
    from El Salvador 233
Remembering Mike 77
What Happened to My American
    Dream? 26

Rape/Date Rape
Dream Guy, Nightmare Experience
    180
He Won't Stop Hitting Me 177
Letters to Parents 169
My Love, My Friend, My Enemy
    185

Relationships
The Anger Can Go Somewhere
    Else 202
Dream Guy, Nightmare Experience
    180
He Won't Stop Hitting Me 177
I Never Thought He'd Try to Kill
    Me 196
I Paid a High Price for Love 171
Letters to Parents 169
My Love, My Friend, My Enemy
    185
My Terrible Secret: Breaking the
    Silence 49

Self-Defense
I Carry Mace . . . Just in Case 125
Why I Carry a Gun 119
Why I Don't Have a Gun 122

Sexual Harassment
Tell Him Why 164
Tired of Being a Target 157
Why Guys Talk Nasty 161

Suicide
I Hated Myself 132
I Never Thought He'd Try to Kill
    Me 196

Weapons
I Carry Mace . . . Just in Case 125
Why I Carry a Gun 119
Why I Don't Have a Gun 122

Young Men
The Anger Can Go Somewhere
    Else 202
Gaybashers: What Are They Trying
    to Prove? 99
Hoods n' the Boys 108
I Hated Myself 132
Rikers: Frontin' for Respect 216
Why Guys Talk Nasty 161

Young Women
I Carry Mace . . . Just in Case 125
I Paid a High Price for Love 171
My Terrible Secret: Breaking the
    Silence 49
Tell Him Why 164
Tired of Being a Target 157
Women Are Under a Rap Attack 91

Acknowledgments

The stories in this book would not exist without the courage and sensitivity of a great number of teenagers whose work does not appear here. For nearly two decades, the young writers of the magazines *New Youth Connections* and *Foster Care Youth United* have come together in a little office in New York City—mostly after school and during their vacations—and together helped to create a unique environment where it is okay to be an individual, to bare your soul, your scars, and to admit that you don't have all the answers. Many of their most urgent stories weren't written down at all or failed to see print. Often the material was just too close or the circumstances of their lives too overwhelming. But the openness of so many of these brave young writers and the tremendous commitment and support they have shown for their peers is what made every piece in this book possible. (They've also taught the editors most of what we know about violence and youth.) The magazines' teen readers also deserve thanks for their years of devotion, their letters to the editor, and their participation in our annual "Letters to Parents" writing contest.

Besides the editors, several other adults were instrumental in drawing out and shaping individual stories included here: Duffie Cohen ("Home Is Where the Hurt Is"), Rachel Blustain ("What Happened to My American Dream?"), and Carol Kelly ("My Terrible Secret").

Youth Communication's work is sustained by the generosity of many foundations, corporations, individuals, and others. The list is too long for this space, but a few deserve special mention. In 1990, the New York Foundation funded a special supplement on "Violence and Conflict Resolution" where two of these stories first appeared. Two years later, a special reprint was commissioned by then New York Mayor David N. Dinkins's Stop the Violence Fund. The Aaron Diamond Foundation, another major supporter, then asked us to develop yet another collection for a "Target: Violence" conference of the New York Regional Association of Grantmakers. This was the first time anyone had expressed an interest in reaching an adult audience with our material on the topic.

In 1995, the *Harvard Educational Review* published several of our stories in a special issue on "Violence and Youth." Around the same time, literary agent Anne Edelstein looked at our proposal for a book and took us under her wing. The editors would also like to thank our editors at Simon & Schuster: Becky Saletan, for her clear vision and light touch and for respecting these young writers and their abilities, and Denise Roy, who approached the project with sensitivity and thoroughness.

About
Youth Communication

Youth Communication is a nonprofit youth development program located in New York City whose mission is to teach writing, journalism, and leadership skills. The teenagers we train, most of whom are New York City public high school students, become writers for our two teen-written publications, *New Youth Connections,* a general-interest youth magazine, and *Foster Care Youth United,* a magazine by and for young people in foster care.

Youth Communication was founded in 1980 by Keith Hefner in response to a nationwide study which found that censorship, mediocrity, and racial exclusion had crippled the high school press. Hefner is the recipient of a Charles H. Revson Fellowship on the Future of the City of New York from Columbia University and the Luther P. Jackson Excellence in Education Award of the New York Association of Black Journalists. In 1989 he won a MacArthur Fellowship for his work at Youth Communication.

Each year, more than one hundred young people participate in Youth Communication's school-year and summer journalism workshops, where they work under the direction of several full-time adult editors. They come from every corner of New York

City, and most are African American, Latino, or Asian. Many are recent immigrants. For these writers, the opportunity to reach their peers with accurate portrayals of their lives and important self-help information motivates them to create powerful stories.

Teachers, counselors, social workers, and other adults circulate our magazines to young people in their classes and after-school youth programs. They distribute 70,000 copies of *New Youth Connections* each month during the school year, and 10,000 bi-monthly copies of *Foster Care Youth United.* Teachers and counselors tell us that the teens they work with—including many who are ordinarily resistant to reading—clamor for these publications. Teen readers report that the information and inspiration in our stories help them reflect on their lives and open lines of communication with parents and teachers.

Running a strong youth development program while simultaneously producing quality teen magazines requires us to be sensitive to the complicated lives and emotions of the teen participants while also providing an intellectually rigorous experience. We achieve that goal in the writing/teaching/editing relationship, which is the core of our program.

Our teaching and editorial process begins with discussions between adult editors and the teen staff, during which they seek to discover the stories that are most important to each teen writer and that will also appeal to a significant segment of our readers.

Once topics have been chosen, students begin the process of crafting their stories. For a personal story, that means revisiting events in one's past to understand their significance for the future. For a commentary, it means developing a logical and persuasive point of view. For a reported story, it means gathering information through research and interviews. Students look inward and outward as they try to make sense of their experiences and the world around them and find the points of intersection between personal and social concerns. That process can take a few weeks or a few months. Stories frequently go through four, five, or more drafts as students work under the guidance of their editors, the way any professional writer does.

Many of the students who walk through our doors have uneven skills, as a result of poor education, living under extremely stressful conditions, or coming from homes where English is a second language. Yet, to complete their stories, students must successfully perform a wide range of activities, including writing and rewriting, reading, discussion, reflection, research, interviewing, and typing. They must work as members of a team and they must accept a great deal of individual responsibility. They learn to verify facts and cope with rejection. They engage in explorations of truthfulness and fairness. They meet deadlines. They must develop the audacity to believe that they have something important to say and the humility to recognize that saying it well is not a process of instant gratification, but usually requires a long, hard struggle through many discussions and much rewriting.

It would be impossible to teach these skills and dispositions as separate, disconnected topics, like grammar, ethics, or assertiveness. However, we find that students make rapid progress when they are learning skills in the context of an inquiry that is personally significant to them and that they think will benefit their peers.

Writers usually participate in our program for one semester, though some stay much longer. Years later, many of them report that working here was a turning point in their lives—that it helped them acquire the confidence and skills that they needed for success in their subsequent education and careers. Scores of our graduates have overcome tremendous obstacles to become journalists, writers, and novelists. Hundreds more are working in law, teaching, business, and other careers. Many former Youth Communication teen staffers have made careers of writing, including National Book Award finalist Edwidge Danticat (*Krik? Krak!*), novelist James Earl Hardy (*B-Boy Blues*), memoirist and editor Veronica Chambers (*Mama's Girl*), and *New York Times* reporter Rachel Swarns.

For information about our publications and programs, write to Youth Communication, 224 West 29th Street, 2nd floor, New York, NY 10001. Contributions to Youth Communication are tax deductible to the fullest extent of the law.

About the Editors

Philip Kay was an editor of *New Youth Connections,* the magazine where all but a few of the stories in this book were originally published, from 1990 to 1997. Prior to coming to Youth Communication, he was a bilingual teacher in a public elementary school in East Harlem and taught Spanish at New York University. Kay received a Revson Fellowship on the Future of the City of New York from Columbia University in 1994. He has a master's degree in Latin American literature and a bachelor's degree from New York University. He teaches journalism part-time at the City University of New York's Hunter College and is currently working on a novel set in New York in the 1980s.

Andrea Estepa was an editor of *New Youth Connections* from 1991 to 1997. Prior to that, she was a reporter for *The Hartford Courant* and the *Los Angeles Times.* In 1997 she was awarded a

Revson Fellowship by Columbia University. Estepa has a master's degree from the School of Journalism at Columbia and a bachelor's degree from Brown University. She is currently working on two collections of writing by and for adolescent girls.

Al Desetta is the editor of *Foster Care Youth United*. From 1985 to 1990, he was an editor of *New Youth Connections* as well as an instructor in Youth Communication's juvenile prison writing program. In 1991, he became the organization's first director of teacher development, working with high school teachers to help them produce better writers and student publications. Prior to working at Youth Communication, Desetta directed environmental education projects in New York City public high schools and worked as a reporter. He has a master's degree in English literature from City College of the City University of New York and a bachelor's degree from the State University of New York at Binghamton, and he was a Revson Fellow at Columbia University for the 1990–91 academic year. He is currently working on a new Youth Communication book that focuses on young people's courage and resilience.

Also by Youth Communication

Starting with "I": Personal Essays by Teenagers (Persea Books, 1997)

The Heart Knows Something Different: Teenage Voices from the Foster Care System (Persea Books, 1995)

Out with It: Gay and Straight Teens Write About Homosexuality (Youth Communication, 1995)